• HALSGROVE DISCOVER SERIES ➤

ROSAMUNDE PILCHER'S CORNWALL

Bret Hawthorne

HALSGROVE

TO RACHEL
who drove the car

ROSAMUNDE PILCHER
1924 – 2019
Thanks for helping me to discover Cornwall

First published in Great Britain in 2019

British Library Cataloguing-in-Publication Data
A CIP record for this title is available from the British Library

ISBN 978 0 85704 312 2

HALSGROVE
Halsgrove House,
Ryelands Business Park,
Bagley Road, Wellington, Somerset TA21 9PZ
Tel: 01823 653777   Fax: 01823 216796
email: sales@halsgrove.com

Information on all Halsgrove titles is available at:
www.halsgrove.com

Printed and bound in India by Parksons Graphics

CONTENTS

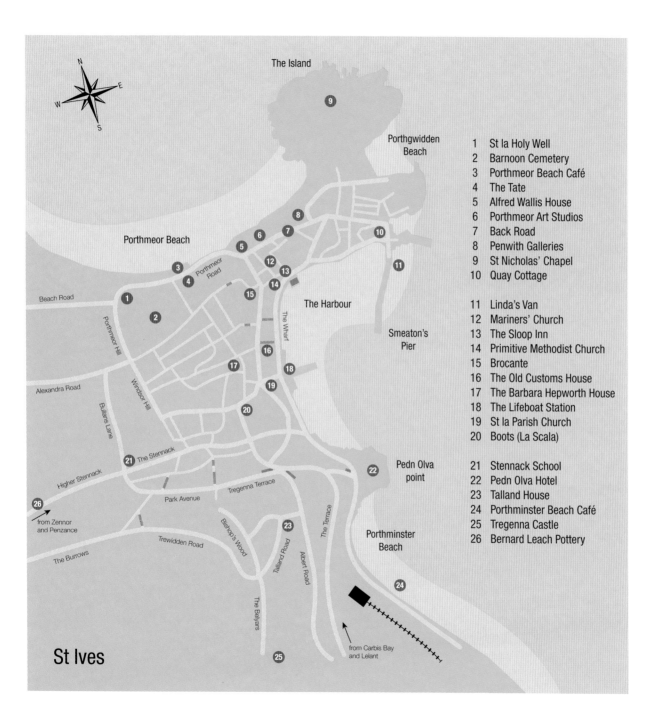

The Island

Porthgwidden
Beach

Porthmeor Beach

Porthmeor Beach

Beach Road

Porthmeor Road

Porthmeor Hill

Alexandra Road

Windsor Hill

Bullans Lane

The Stennack

Higher Stennack

Park Avenue

Tregenna Terrace

Trewidden Road

The Burrows

Bishop's Wood

The Belyars

Talland Road

Albert Road

The Terrace

The Wharf

The Harbour

Smeaton's
Pier

Pedn Olva
point

Porthminster
Beach

from Zennor
and Penzance

from Carbis Bay
and Lelant

St Ives

1	St Ia Holy Well
2	Barnoon Cemetery
3	Porthmeor Beach Café
4	The Tate
5	Alfred Wallis House
6	Porthmeor Art Studios
7	Back Road
8	Penwith Galleries
9	St Nicholas' Chapel
10	Quay Cottage
11	Linda's Van
12	Mariners' Church
13	The Sloop Inn
14	Primitive Methodist Church
15	Brocante
16	The Old Customs House
17	The Barbara Hepworth House
18	The Lifeboat Station
19	St Ia Parish Church
20	Boots (La Scala)
21	Stennack School
22	Pedn Olva Hotel
23	Talland House
24	Porthminster Beach Café
25	Tregenna Castle
26	Bernard Leach Pottery

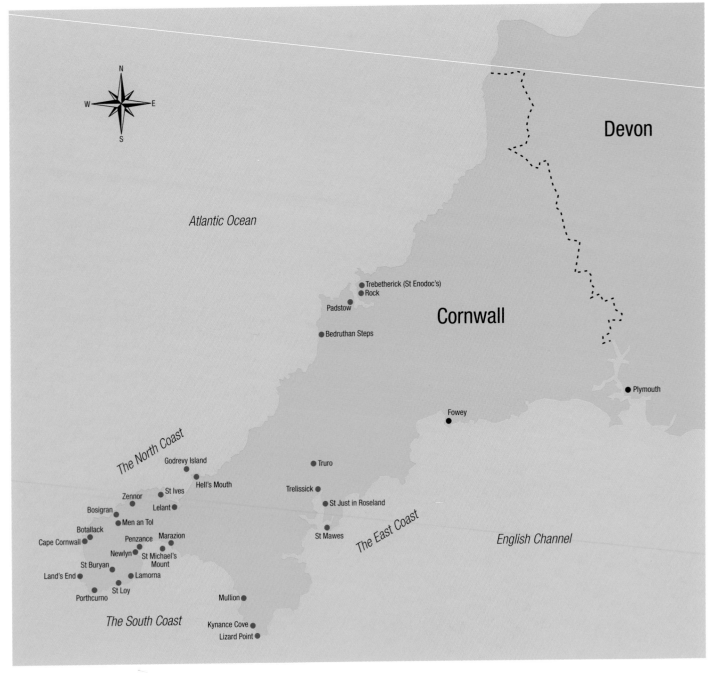

1

ENCHANTING CORNWALL

Introduction

I suppose I got my love of books – my wife would probably say my obsession – from my father. He was a teacher and, as a child, I was surrounded by books: in English, in French, in German, books in Russian. He also had his name down with the local library, and received entire collections from members who had moved on to borrow from that great librarian in the sky.

There was one old paper-back amongst them that particularly fascinated me. Its covers and pages were dog-eared and browned from too much sun and too much use: it had clearly been a trusty companion to its owner. *Through the Window – Paddington to Penzance* was first published by the Great Western Railway Company in 1924. It describes the 305 miles of countryside that the Cornish Riviera Express steams through on its way towards Cornwall.

A journey, according to the author, which has about it a spice of adventure, a certain savour of mysticism and romance. A journey to a land of mists and legends – with its own identity unlike anywhere else in England. To paraphrase a famous opening line, "Cornwall is a foreign country: they do things differently there".

*   *   *

Rosamunde Pilcher was born in Cornwall, in Lelant, near St Ives. Aged just twenty-two, she traded the sky-blue climes of her home for the harsher, greyer landscape of Dundee in the east of Scotland, to be at her new husband's side. But she would keep returning to the light, warmth and colours of Cornwall, if only in her writing.

She writes, above all, of St Ives (in her books, Porthkerris): its houses, alleys, harbour and artists. As a backdrop, she gives us the many and varied landscapes of Penwith (the most western of the Cornish hundreds) – the people; the countryside and flowers; the moors, coast, cliffs and coves. With an artist's eye, she describes the ever-changing interplay of sky, sea and light that this part of the country is renowned for.

St Ives, the Light (1) – crisp and clear

St Ives, the Light (2) – soft and subdued

St Ives, the Light (3) – bright and brooding

*   *   *

For many years I lived abroad. When I returned, Devon became my home again. I came to know East Cornwall – Fowey and its surroundings – through family holidays and my reading of Daphne du Maurier. Like so many others, I had day-tripped to St Ives. But, in my mind, there still remained those childhood imaginings of that mystical, Celtic promontory reaching out into the Atlantic Ocean. Over the years, my original ideas had, in a process of "crystallisation" (to use a term coined by Stendhal), acquired various modifications and embellishments: TV-celebrity and Michelin-starred chefs; alternative lifestyles; the whole surfing set-up; and above all, my growing appreciation of the international importance and influence of the Penwith artists and sculptors.

*   *   *

Spring Bank Holiday, May 2018. Today, fresh from my reading of Rosamunde Pilcher's novels – charting her rise from conventional "romantic" Mills and Boon debutante to best-selling author of family sagas and relationships in *The Shell Seekers and Coming Home* – we are off to discover the different faces of Cornwall that appear in so much of her work. A week to visit all those places I have heard and read about; to explore their presents and uncover their pasts. Not least, an interesting experiment to see if reality really can match up to such long-held expectations.

Despite the gloomy forecasts, the sun is shining. The road-side verges are a pyrotechnical display of red, mauve, and pink rhododendrons with torches of white hawthorn bursting through. Further west, the hawthorns will be bent and stooped like geriatric twig brooms – a reminder of the power of the Atlantic gales. A mile or so later, and an outlandishly exotic tree with long, bright, red-orange catkins is overhanging a wall. Cornwall is a place of contrasts.

Landrake, Trerulefoot, Polzeath, Penzance – place names are linguistic time-capsules: custodians of the last vestiges of the Cornish language, which, in turn, had evolved from the ancient Celtic tongue of its forbears.[1]

Engine houses and chimneys of abandoned mines dot the landscape as we approach Camborne – on the banks of rivers, next to the roadside, way off on the hills on the horizon. These, too, remnants, but of a not so distant past.

Back to the present. It's a bright, hazy day as we drive down the broad highway that crosses the River Hayle. A motorbike, doing at least 100 miles per hour, roars past us and is gone. And now, ahead of us, on the horizon, we can make out the blue of the sea, shimmering in the sunshine.

Kernow a'gas dynergh! Welcome to Cornwall!

Bret Hawthorne

On Seeing St Ives for the First Time

"Roofs of houses, faded slate and whitewashed chimneys, tumbled without pattern or order down the hill. Here a blue door, here a yellow window; here a window-sill bright with geraniums, a line of washing gay as flags, or the leaves of some unsuspected and normally unseen tree. Beyond the roofs and far below them was the harbour, at full tide and sparkling with sunshine. Boats rocked at anchor and a white sail sped beyond the shelter of the harbour wall, heading for the ruler line of the horizon where the two blues met."

Another View, **Rosamunde Pilcher.** © Rosamunde Pilcher. Reproduced by permission of Hodder and Stoughton Limited

That first sight of the town is unique in the whole of the country. Like Pilcher, Betjeman enthused over it; Hepworth was reminded of "Mediterranean light and colour, which so excites one's sense of form". Be it summer, with the tide out and holiday-makers walking from the harbour to Porthminster across the golden expanse of sands; be it autumn with an easterly blowing and waves crashing over the harbour wall – the view, in the sunshine, never fails to take your breath away.

As I will discover this week, it really is all about the light here in St Ives. You will have read that so many times, but it's a fact – in the lux department, the town has been remarkably blessed.

J. M. W. Turner was the first painter to be drawn, for this reason, to the town in 1811, returning again in 1813. There then followed a whole succession of artists, some passing through, others deciding, in the end, to make St Ives their home. Amongst their number, Whistler, with his disciple Sickert; Holman Hunt, the Pre-raphaelite; Olsson, the master of seascapes; Hepworth, Nicholson and Bernard Leach; Rothko – even Francis Bacon paid a visit. Pilcher readers might add to that list Ben Lytton and Laurence Stern.

St Ives, the Light (4) – silver and shimmering

St Ives in June

St Ives in October

I hop out to catch the image on camera. From this vantage point and others around the town, three main landmarks command your attention above all: the Chapel of St Nicholas, on the headland, looking out over the waves; the tower of the church of St Ia, keeping watch over her flock; and far over to the east, in the distance, the small white tower of Godrevy Lighthouse, standing guard over the approaches to the bay.

(Left) St Nicholas' Chapel and (Right) Godrevy Lighthouse

(Below) Quay Cottage

I regain the car, to hear words from my wife, Rachel, for the situation I have put her in vis-à-vis the irate drivers backed up behind, and soon we are descending the narrow streets, lined with buff-coloured granite buildings, that lead into town.

Our base for this week, Quay Cottage, is on the far-side of the harbour. We take the passage down by the side of the church (closed today I notice) and take a left at the lifeboat station onto the waterfront. The crowds of bank-holiday visitors, spilling from the pavements into the road, impose their own pace on the motorists. Perhaps I am running ahead of myself here, but the situation we find ourselves in (my driver might not agree with me on this) in a way sums up the Cornish experience. What I mean is, Cornwall invites you, encourages you, to slow down; to relax; to take life at a calmer, more leisurely tempo, which is why a holiday here is so appealing to city-dwellers. In this instance, it gives me time, as we edge cautiously forward, to observe tourists lining up for ice-cream; boat trip vendors; and shoppers selecting souvenirs to take back home.

(Left) St Ia

The Sloop Inn, which seems a familiar friend already, after all the reading I have done on St Ives prior to arrival, marks the angle of the L-shape that Wharf Road describes around the harbour. Next comes an Italian restaurant followed by a speciality gin bar.

Then, an even slower stretch – cars, parents, children and dogs all funnelling into a narrow section with houses on both sides. There's another ice cream kiosk with statutory queue and on the left a giant emporium, an Aladdin's cave of all things beach: buckets, spades, rings, lilos and kayaks. And, finally, there it is – the house; with a courtyard garden, unheard of down by the harbour.

We don't even bother to check if there are spaces in the recommended Island car park on a packed day like this. We have, during our twenty-minute drive around the harbour, spotted a parking space, a slot, on Smeaton's Pier – the iconic wall with its two lighthouses, the barrier between the boats and the sea beyond. More expensive, but really handy for the luggage. Rachel starts back towards the cottage while I go round to the boot to gather up books and maps, before bringing the main case over.

"I can't see over your back end!" – a disembodied voice from the other side of the car.

I walk round and realise we have chosen a space quite close to an old red camper van.

"The way you're parked – I can't see what I'm painting anymore"

The side doors of the camper are open, framing a rather annoyed-looking lady with grey hair, spectacles, a sun visor, and dressed in an old paint-spattered apron. She is clutching a good twenty or so brushes and sitting on a folding stool planted in the middle of a small Persian carpet, a large canvas in front of her; the easel half in, half out of the door, and surrounded by innumerable rags, crumpled tubes of paint, sheets and boxes.

(Above) The Lifeboat Station

(Below) Boat trip?

The Old Custom's House

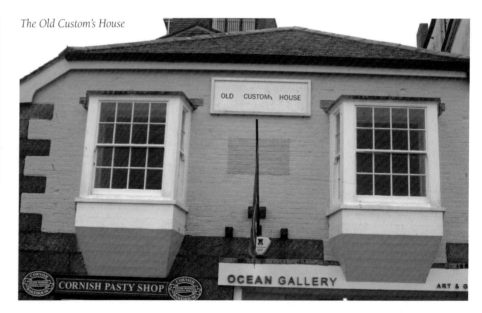

(Left) The Sloop Inn

(Right) The harbour beach

I suggest turning the car around so she can look out over the bonnet. Easier said. Turning our large car round on the narrow quay, avoiding bollards, nets, anchors and holiday-makers involves an infinite number of backward and forward manoeuvres. Ten minutes later, I descend to see if the new position meets with approval. It seems to.

I explain we are here so I can take some photos for a book that I am writing.

"So you're an illustrator?" "Er, yes, I'm taking photos for a book I am writing" (not an illustrator where I come from). "Yes, I got that" she answers pointedly.

I try another tack. The painting – a large canvas of the harbour – is not at all displeasing in a naïf sort of way. I ask how much a painting like that might sell for. "Maybe 2000. 500, if I'm hard up" – and there is a glint in her eye.

13

The lady in the van, as we come to call her, is called Linda and lives above the church. Talk turns to parking and she tells me she leaves the van here most of the time. Then somehow we get on to talking about family and children, and how my son, Nick, lives in Barcelona and here – this is Rachel my wife. Rachel has come back to look for me concerned that it could take over twenty-five minutes to get one suitcase out of a car.

I introduce her to Linda who tells her she already knows all about her, much to Rachel's amusement.

As one of the main reasons for coming to St Ives is to find out about the art and artists, to meet one just as we arrive seems auspicious. We take our leave of Linda who kindly offers to keep an eye on the car. Our daily chats about the weather; the parking; the locals – everybody is very trusting; places to eat and the like, will be a looked-forward-to feature of the coming week.

The Lady in the Van – Linda

2

IN THE BEGINNING

Lelant

Rosamunde Pilcher was born in the town of Lelant, on the Hayle Estuary, on Monday, 22 September 1924. On the birth certificate her name is recorded as Rosamunde Evelina Montague Laurence Scott. Montague and Laurence are her father Charles' middle names. Evelina is from a paternal grandmother. Her father's profession is Port Surveyor of Rangoon.

She was born at a boarding house, Chilecito Villas, in Uny Lelant. The Villas (the owner was clearly proud of his three-house terrace) were built in 1903 by a successful miner upon his return from South America. Chilecito is, in fact, a mining village in the North East of Argentina, just the other side of the Andes from Chile. From there, a cable car, built in 1904 by a German company, connects with La Mejicana gold mine high up in the mountains. The 40-kilometre ride takes you up through the clouds to a height of 4500 metres where the mine is located. The name Chilecito – little Chile – is down to the fact that almost all of the miners were of Chilean origin, leaving their own country to find work – just as happened in Cornwall.

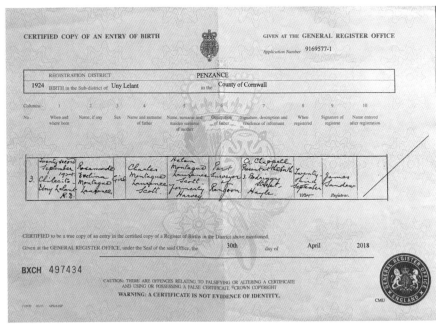

Rosamunde Pilcher's birth certificate

Somewhere in my research I had also discovered that a midwife was connected with the villas. In a place as remote as Cornwall was in the early 1920s, this was a good person for Pilcher's mother to have around.

(Left) Chilecito Villas, Lelant

(Right) Chilecito Villas, 1903

What else was happening in the world in 1924?

Well, some things were just the same as ever. US Presidential candidate John Davis was vigorously condemning the Ku Klux Klan; the Prince of Wales, on a tour of North America, joined a fox-hunt in Toronto; and the H. J. Heinz Company was celebrating its fifty-fifth birthday.

Some things were new: Malcom Campbell had just set a world landspeed record. The French marked up the furthest distance to date for a flight by helicopter (360 metres) and, on 15 October, the first Surrealist manifesto was published.

The old world order was changing. There was rioting in Burma for home rule led by a Buddhist priest and meanwhile, on the sub-continent, Mahatma Ghandi was fasting in a despairing protest over the recent Hindu-Muslim riots.

Some things, however, were even more ominous: the Spanish were having a trial-run dictatorship with Miguel Primo de Rivera, while, across the water, Benito Mussolini was launching his grandiose, new architectural projects in Rome.

Lelant Station platform

The Dawes plan – dealing with Germany's reparations for the First World War – had been put into action. In 1929, however, even the best-laid schemes ran right into the Wall Street crash. A world recession ensued. Germany was faced with hyperinflation, 40 per cent unemployment and could no longer make her agreed repayments. The country started to look to new leadership to guide them out of the mess. At the moment of Rosamunde Pilcher's birth in that September of 1924, a sequence of events was already under way that would lead inexorably to the global conflict situations described in the The Shell Seekers and Coming Home.

Shortly after her daughter was born, her mother moved Rosamunde and her sister, Lalage (five years older), to a semi-detached Edwardian house, closer to the centre of the village, and overlooking the estuary. The house stands just up from pretty Lelant Station on the branch line from St Erth to St Ives.

At this time, St Ives was still a smelly fishing village. Lelant (Penmarron in *Coming Home*), on the other hand, could boast a links golf course, home to the West Cornwall Golf Club. It had been founded in 1889, by the artist, Adrian Stokes. Jim Barnes, the US and British Open winner, a Lelant local, played at the club in the early 1900s. Reminiscences of folk living in Lelant at the time talk of two sets of people: the ones in the big houses, and the ones who served them – in their dining rooms, in their kitchens or in the shops.

A documentary by BBC Scotland about the writer's life shows her in front of the garden of the house – the gate is even the same one she knew as a child. She lived there for twelve years, until her father returned from the Far East. The house was called The Elms – it's the house on the left as you look up from the road. In *Coming Home*, the house is called Riverview.

It is possible to stay at The Firs, a boutique waterside B & B, which forms the other side of the semi-detached house I have seen in the film. Their website offers prospective clients a choice of two bedrooms: The Blue Bedroom or The Shell Seekers, and, it goes on, this is the home where Rosamunde Pilcher spent her childhood and grew up.

West Cornwall Golf Club

(Left) The gate to The Elms

(Right) The Firs – Boutique waterside B & B

17

(Above) The view from The Firs gate up to the house

(Right) Typical drawing room furniture 1926

I decide to phone, and I speak to Marie, the owner. I ask about the two sides of the house and tell her about the documentary. Marie tells me that Pilcher did actually live at The Firs, but the then owner of the house did not want to appear in the film, and so the next door neighbour from The Elms stood in.

That seems plausible, and she should know, and anyway it's not as if they are separate houses. Staying in The Shell Seekers (at The Firs) you wake up with the exact same view as Judith Dunbar had every morning, which for a Pilcher fan must be the tops. Marie is very kind and helpful, and I decide I will definitely book in one night in the future. Although she is away, she will allow me to pop over the next day to take some photos of the house and garden.

We park outside the station, and walk under the arching passage of trees towards the house. This road forms the initial section of St Michael's Way, and has recently become part of the official Camino de Santiago. Pilgrims, arriving from Ireland, would take this route across the Penwith peninsula to Mounts Bay from where they could board a ship bound for Compostela in Spain to indulgently venerate the relics of the scallop-encrusted Saint James.

We open the gate and walk up the terraced garden. It's a big house. Rosamunde Pilcher complains that as a child it was cold; that they lived on a shoe-string; and that with her father away her mother found holding the fort not an easy job. But then this was definitely not slumming it, and it was the 1930s with a depression on… and her mother was bringing them up on her own.

We turn to look back over the estuary. Obscured by the curtain of trees, the squeaking of brakes announces the arrival of a train into the station. Apparently, in the book, as in real life, the train driver would wait for the young Pilcher who, late getting ready for school, would be running down the garden path.

"Lelant. A seaport in the Middle Ages, until outdone by St Ives". Twelve words – concise, even for Mr Pevsner. (Pevsner's *Cornwall* in his *Buildings of England* series is one of the guides I have brought along with me – more about him later.) We drive along Church Road to see his only entry for the town: the church of St Uny. Its south door has, we read, "nice fleurons in jambs and voussoirs and tracery decoration in the spandrels" (don't worry, Pevsner provides a glossary). As elsewhere in Cornwall, clear as to their priorities, the locals have decided to surround the church with a golf course. Pilcher was christened here but because of her mother's religious leanings; she never attended from then on. She would return, however, on her wedding day in 1946.

(Above) The railway line is just behind the trees across the road

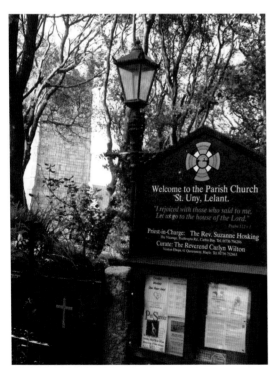

The parish church of St Uny, Lelant

The church from the graveyard

19

Hayle Towans

We pass between the two halves of the churchyard down a sunken path (I think we are now crossing a fairway), past World War Two gun emplacements and under the railway line out on to the wide expanse of Hayle Towans (towans = dunes in Cornish) and Porth Kidney beach. This is where the young Rosamunde Pilcher would play on her own and make up stories.

Lelant hadn't so much been outdone by St Ives, rather its port had been completely overrun by the sand and dunes in front of us – a phenomenon with which St Ives would also have to do battle.

Pilcher had also mentioned in the documentary that she only lived at the house until she was twelve, when her father returned from the Far East. Doing a bit of detective work, nosing about on Findmypast, I am invited to check out the 1939 register, an exhaustive list of all persons in the country at the outbreak of war. I type in Scott, Lelant. The Scott Household comes up (three people); two of the records are closed, but one – Helen Scott, DOB 24 July 1888, married – is open. The address is Green Lockning, Church Road.

The internet tells me there is no Green Lockning, but there is a Green Loaning (a Scottish name from a song about Flodden, a "loan" being a lane or field) and the second entry tells me that it is for sale through the estate agency, Savills. "A charming and well-designed family home, in need of some modernisation. five bedrooms and set in a generous plot … and was, from circa 1934, the childhood home of author Rosamunde Pilcher. Guide price £595,000."

Then, scrolling down, there's an entry from *Kelly's Directory* of 1939: CML Scott, Commander Royal Navy, retired, Green Loaning. At this point, a thought crosses my mind: for a young girl who

Hayle Towans, back in the day

so missed her absent father in her childhood, how must she have felt when he does return and she has already been sent away to boarding school in Penzance?

But there's something else. Another entry for *The London Gazette*, 15 January 1955, impersonally informs us that Helen Scott of Green Loaning passed away, on 25 December 1954. Christmas Day. At the age of sixty-six. The same age as Penelope Keeling when she died in *The Shell Seekers*.

Again in the same BBC Scotland documentary, talking about the novel *Winter Solstice*, Pilcher had, in fact, said, in a wistful and enigmatic tone, "Christmas is not my favourite time of the year, actually". Now I understand why. And is that why, so often – in *Coming Home*, for example – she creates fictional Happy Christmases for her characters to enjoy? To rewrite the hurt?

But to return to *The Shell Seekers* – I had read all the preceding novels but found this one was somehow different from the others, this one seemed to "ring truer". It was more personal, more written from the heart. And the take on the mother figure, Penelope, had changed. This was no longer an unkind, prying character resented by the daughter. This was a mother portrayed by an author who realised a mother has her own life – beyond the bringing up of children – with all its joys and sorrows. This must be Pilcher's own mature revisiting, as a mother herself, of the relationship she had had

Green Loaning

Church Lane, Lelant, in 1930

Paddington Station. The Cornish Riviera Express (see pages 7 and 85) always left from Platform 1

with her own mother. Something of Helen Scott, seen in a new light, had been put into the creating of Penelope.

I'm not sure if I should have, but I decide to find out what other parallels there are between Penelope and Pilcher's mother. Penelope, we know from the start of the book, has a heart condition – when we meet her on the very first page, she's in a taxi returning from the hospital after a suspected heart attack. You are aware of the illness hanging over proceedings throughout the novel. In the end, her heart does, in fact, give out.

I apply for a copy of her mother's death certificate. I think I knew what I would see before I opened the envelope containing the document. There it was: "Cause of death: ventricular tachycardia."

No wonder the events of the novel felt personal and real.

This, in turn, threw up another possibly interesting line of enquiry. I had always been puzzled why – from the publication of *The Brown Fields* in 1951, until 10 books later, *A Long Way from Home* in 1963 – Pilcher had always written under the pseudonym of Jane Fraser – with one exception. In 1955 – the year after her mother dies – she has a change of tack and *A Secret to Tell* is published under her own name. Was there some secret revelation that the book contained, which she couldn't tell before?

The book is not to be found anywhere: not on Amazon, nor Abe Books, nor with specialist second-hand sellers. Finally, with a visit to London planned to see the Summer Exhibition, after arriving in Paddington station, I take the opportunity to divert briefly to the British Library to solve the mystery. My photo and details taken, and card issued, I can proceed to the reading room for the viewing.

No startling revelations, I'm afraid. It's a romance, set in South Africa, with a bit of a James Bond action slant – disappointing. I can only think that, as her mother had poured scorn on her writing, she had dropped the subterfuge adopted till then and taken the first opportunity to put her real name to something. Probably even she realised the quality wasn't the best, and better to wait a little longer before going public.

Not a completely wasted journey, however. Visiting the British Library is an experience in itself and I now have a distinctive British Library pencil to boot.

Nancherrow I

There were four houses, then, in Pilcher's childhood: Chilecito Villas, The Elms/Firs, Green Loaning and a fictitious one, Nancherrow. Nancherrow is the manor house owned by Judith Dunbar's adoptive family, the Carey-Lewises, in the novel *Coming Home*.

I have located the first three, but just where was Nancherrow exactly? In the documentary, Pilcher, talking in Lelant, is asked about the real-life location of the house. "It was on the other side", she cryptically replies.Midway through the film, the camera cuts to the façade of an old manor house with mullion windows. It could date from the latter part of the seventeenth century. It's not your Manderley-type – it's too irregular, too rambling. It's a modest house, a world away from the stately pile of Wrotham Park, Hertfordshire, chosen by the German film-crew in the film *Nancherrow* with Ms Lumley and co.

Pilcher enters stage left and stops on the gravel path in front of the porch and says to camera that this was the inspiration for Nancherrow. She was invited here as a child on several occasions to play with the other children. She says the man who used to own the house liked entertaining and there were always lots of interesting and beautiful people about but that the children always just wanted to dash off down to the cove.

This involved going down a path, past a farm, through a disused quarry, over a stile to the sea. Exactly as it is described in *Coming Home*.

Gunnera, that monstruous prickly-stemmed plant

"*The path narrowed and plunged downwards into a jungle of semi–tropical vegetation; camellias, late-flowering hydrangeas, stately rhododendrons, lush clumps and thickets of bamboo and tall-stemmed palms…Then a stream appeared from the undergrowth of creeping ivy and moss and fern and bubbled and tumbled its way down a rocky bed, alongside where they walked. From time to time the path crossed and re-crossed the flowing water, by means of ornamental wooden bridges … She looked and saw that, ahead, the sloping path plunged into a cavern of gunnera, that monstrous prickly-stemmed plant, with leaves large as umbrellas… they climbed the bank and then the gate, and jumped down onto the tarmac of a narrow farm road. On the far side of this was a low drystone wall, and then, finally there were the cliffs and the sea… The sun was out, the sea intensely blue, flecked with white-caps… Gulls hung screaming overhead, and the thunder of the waves was continuous.*"

Coming Home, Rosamunde Pilcher. © Rosamunde Pilcher. Reproduced by permission of Hodder and Stoughton Limited

It sounds just like one of those semi-tropical National Trust gardens that the county is so famous for. I will return many times to passages like this in the coming months, as the quest for the house gradually becomes the bane of my research.

Pilcher meets the Lady of the Manor, the current owner. They are standing in a walled, French-style garden, unusual for Cornwall. Then she meets a group of people: farm workers or gardeners, and signs copies of their Pilcher books.

The film ends, but the name of the house has not been mentioned, and the documentary has no credits.

The name itself, Nancherrow, I discover, comes from a village just outside St Just but that is not where the house is located.

I scour the whole of the Penwith peninsula, nay west Cornwall, with Google Earth, looking out for the distinctive garden but draw a blank. If the truth be told, it's a bit like searching for a needle in your proverbial haystack. I will keep you posted regarding my search as this book unfolds.

3

FROM *WOMAN AND HOME* MAGAZINE TO *NEW YORK TIMES* BESTSELLER

Family Background

Pilcher's mother, Helen, had been born in the Orkneys. Her family then moved to Glasgow. Pilcher presumes that it was here that she met her father Charles Scott, who was in the Royal Navy. They were married in Hong Kong Cathedral. In 1924, her father found a job in charge of the dredging of the River Irrawaddy at Rangoon, keeping the channels clear for the boats sailing down from Mandalay with teak and rubies.

By this time, Pilcher's mother was already pregnant with her second child and made the decision not to follow him on to Burma. On a whim, she decides to settle in a place she had been on holiday to as a girl in Cornwall.

St Ives, Porthmeor Beach

That her parents' situation – her father being away, her mother left behind to bring up two children on her own – affected Rosamunde Pilcher deeply, is clear from the way the almost obsessive themes of separation, divorce, and children growing up alone and fending for themselves, are so recurrent throughout the novels. Writing was perhaps a way of coming to terms with the feelings, of sorting things out in her head.

Her novels will revolve around one dominant theme – an absent, or distant (either geographically or by age) male or father figure, with a mother being (unconsciously?) blamed for this state of affairs.

There is a constant longing to go back to where one grew up and perhaps find that missing person. A search for acceptance, a need to set up a home, find home – come home. And with this comes a sensation that her characters express on several occasions: an insecurity, stemming from the sensation that there are two worlds – an ideal-one, searched for, and a real-one, lived in. Two worlds which almost, but don't quite, touch.

Mother-figures, especially, don't fare so well in the novels. They can be domineering, cold and controlling – not thinking twice about interfering in their daughter's lives and futures if the daughter's plans don't line up with the mother's ambitions. Only at the end of *The Empty House*, for example, does Virginia discover that her mother had taken and ripped up letters from Eustace, a boyfriend she had disapproved of. Mothers are believed and relied on but can sometimes prove "downright untrustworthy" (the exact words used by Pilcher to describe her own mother).

Pilcher's mother thought her young daughter's stories "stupid". Compliments and praise were practically non-existent. When she started writing for Mills and Boon, and various women's magazines such as *Woman's Weekly*, her mother was "very scathing about the whole thing". And controlling – a Christian Scientist who, when the child was ill with earache, whooping cough or running a temperature, would refuse to let her see a doctor.

Pilcher does manage a "but" – but it is a "but" so steeped in faint praise as to be practically worthless. It was her mother who brought her to Cornwall, and had it not been for this inspired decision, none of what she has written would ever have happened. For that, at least, she is grateful.

Porthmeor beach, St Ives

Her standpoint on her absent father varies. At times she will say it was not unusual for a father to be away in those days, most families having some male or other out in India, or Malaya, or Africa, planting rubber, doing their bit for the British Empire, or serving in the Armed Forces. And she will claim that never having known her father, she never missed him.

On other occasions, she laments that coming home, as he did, for three or four months only once every four years, she never had time to build a father-daughter relationship, which left her feeling incomplete. Returning from Burma he always brought her presents – and you think of the significance for Judith Dunbar of the wooden chest she receives one Christmas at boarding school in *Coming Home*.

Her father, during his brief presences in England, is the one who encourages her with her writing. A notebook he gives on a car journey aged seven is used to write her very first play. Later, when a Wren in Ceylon, it is her father who submits her very first short story to *Woman and Home* magazine. And it is he who cables to say that it has been published for 15 guineas. The moment she knew she could do it, she recalls.

Fathers, in her work, although often absent, are kindly portrayed, always idealised, given the benefit of the doubt and excused their prolonged disappearances. The strategy is usually to make them mercurial artists, like Ben Litton in *Another View*, or Daniel, the untameable artist in *The Carousel*. They have to be forgiven because of their genius. Her work is littered with benevolent grandfather-artist figures, such as the Commander in *The Day of the Storm* or Laurence Stern in *The Shell Seekers*.

St Ives rooftops seen from The Tate café

And, as happens to Judith, at twelve-years-old Pilcher's mother also leaves, with her sister, for Burma for a whole year.

Enter the surrogate family.

For Judith in *Coming Home* it will be the Carey-Lewises – the parents of Loveday, a fellow boarder – who live at Nancherrow. For the young Rosamunde, it is best friend, Sarah Trembath and her parents Jim and Kitty. (There's still a Trembath House just on the left just outside Newlyn on the road to St Buryan.)

Jim has a car and takes them on picnics; Jim reads *Treasure Island* aloud; Jim leaves a toffee by their beds every night while they sleep. Jim, the father.

The Trembaths – how many of these Trembath traits are familiar to Pilcher readers? They have a house always full of people; a kitchen with a Cornish range; a fire in the grate which is always lit; a gardener who digs the vegetable patch; climbing roses; and mutton stew for tea.

She passes an idyllic year. Christmas is exactly as it should be. Her mother never had a tree, or decorations, naturally.

It is probably useful to remember at this point that these are the memories of a ten-year-old child. Pilcher notes that her own mother – not surprisingly – had become slightly jealous of this other unknown woman and that she was aware of this conflict between the two mothers.

In a magazine article published in 2001, entitled *Roam Alone*, a slightly more realistic version of events emerges. She recounts how her father's prolonged absences must have made it difficult for her mother and their relationship. Rather tense when they were together, their reunions, and Christmases, which one always expected (as a child) to be so magical were invariably a disappointment.

Other comments speak reams about her mother's actual situation. It was left to Mum to look after them and she would protest "I have to do everything round here". With her husband absent, everything had to be run on a shoestring. Although fairly comfortable in Cornwall, there was little money for extras.

Meanwhile, on the other side of the world, her father's home in Burma was a pretty smart place and expensive to run. He always had a driver and staff on hand to help.

Pre-Bestsellers – Mills and Boon territory

You have to admire Rosamunde Pilcher's perseverance and tenacity. Almost forty years were to pass from her first published novel, *Half-Way to the Moon (1949)* until she hit the big-time with *The Shell Seekers* in 1988.

She started out writing for Mills and Boon under the pseudonym of Jane Fraser. A back-cover blurb from the 1950s (with a youthful photo of the real Rosamunde Pilcher) reveals that she was a woman of her time with somewhat modest views as to her worth:

"Now (Jane) is married, she spends most of the time coping with the various needs of a husband, three lovely children and three dogs....She has been up in an aeroplane, down in a submarine, and once made a loose cover for an armchair; these she considers her three greatest achievements"

I know some die-hards will have delved into Pilcher's early Jane Fraser work – I myself (for research purposes) read *Young Bar* (1952) and *The Keeper's House* (1963). They are however, I can assure you, only for the most fanatical fan or for those readers who totally espouse the Mills and Boon approach to literature. I would not recommend them.

Apart from the one-off *A Secret to Tell* (1955), Rosamunde Pilcher only started writing under her own name in 1965 with *On my Own*. By the time she came to write *The Shell Seekers*, twenty-three years and 11 novels later, she had already covered many of the themes the book would contain, including the perils of inheritance, the greed of children and children (who are in fact adults) falling out with each other. The artist grandfather is also present in earlier works. The painting *The Shell Seekers* actually appears in *The Day of the Storm*, described but not named, but this time it's the work of the artist Grenville Bayliss.

However, the millions of new readers who would get their initiation into the Pilcher world with *The Shell Seekers* would only discover this later, as her back catalogue started to become popular. From a practical point of view, it meant that she could reuse these themes as sales of her previous books had not been massive.

The Shell Seekers was painted from one of these studio windows on Porthmeor beach

The Shell Seekers *and* Coming Home

So, 22 novels down the line, if the themes, the descriptions of Cornwall, the cottages, the landscapes, the gardens were all to be found in previous works, just what was it that made *The Shell Seekers* so different? What was it that took her from a cut above sophisticated "romance" novels with a modest readership to a writer about whom her American publisher can say "I think she has sold 50, 60, 70 million books"? (What's 20 million amongst friends anyway?)

For one thing, she listened carefully to her publisher's advice to write a really big, fat read for women. He identifies things Americans like as comfy chairs, fireplaces and dogs (yes, really) but also families of three generations who are still in communication. This was the *Dynasty* and *Dallas* era – huge soapy sagas about the in-fighting of grandparents, parents and children. She also cleverly gives a nod to the American reader by making the hero, the love of Penelope's life, Richard Lomax, an American-in-Cornwall preparing troops for the D-Day landings.

But it's more than that. She has grown-up as a writer. The central character is no longer the usual young girl – a daughter, in her late twenties or thirties – seeing the world through rose-tinted glasses, with problematic mother and nannies, searching for her love of eighteen years ago. The protagonist of *The Shell Seekers*, Penelope, is a mother with three grown children, looking back over her life, while watching her children squabble over a possible inheritance embodied by a painting. This new narrative point of view opens the book up to a completely new audience.

And, above all, the more mature central character has a wealth of experiences and memories she can share. Now a whole new generation of readers can tap into that remembered world.

Coming Home shows how powerful recollections of childhood can be. I think back to my own childhood and things that young people today no longer have any idea about. Bottles of milk on the doorstep, their tops pecked by the birds. Music cassettes that regularly unravelled and had to be wound back in with a pencil. How, in a world without mobile phones, when you went on a date, and the person didn't show up at the agreed time, you had to decide how long you would give them to arrive before you gave up and made your way dejectedly home.

That the past is another country where they do things differently is a quote she uses more than once. *The Shell Seekers* and especially *Coming Home* take us to a place where letters are hand-written on headed notepaper, where there are telegrams, and phones go pip, pip, pip; where you can fly BOAC to an unspoilt Ibiza and find restaurants with chianti bottle lamps. A world where your sandals for the summer have buckles and in the winter there are electric blankets. Gramophones play slightly fuzzy and crackly Charles Trenet songs. If you went to the pictures you watched your film through a haze of cigarette smoke. In fact, forget the flicks – everyone was smoking everywhere – in the posters, on TV, in the house. In the bathroom there were no anti-bacterial gel dispensers – you washed your hands properly with bars of soap. And, when you'd wiped a tear from your eye at the end of *Brief Encounter*, you tucked your hanky up the cuff of your cardigan (which reeked by that point of his Lucky Strikes).

Rosamunde Pilcher's memories as a child growing up in the 1930s are all the more poignant as that generation were unaware that when they got to look back, if indeed they did get to look back, theirs would be the traumatised memories of a generation whose childhood had been ripped apart

Latter-day shell seekers

– in many cases fathers, mothers, uncles, aunts, friends and loved ones lost, scythed down by the conflict of the Second World War.

The Shell Seekers, not surprisingly, is the first novel not to have a *Miracle on 34th Street* ending where everything works out just right, and the happy couple go off into the sunset to tell of their engagement. There is a happy ending, of sorts, but it is a vicarious one for Penelope, lived through the romance of Danus and Antonia. I suppose you could say, yes, she does ultimately get to be with Richard, but not in the way she might have wanted to.

Add to all the above ingredients a heaped spoonful of slightly upper-crust, Bohemian life-style, centred around aga-warmed kitchens; mix in a little plot-suspense regarding lost (or hidden?) immensely valuable sketches, and you have a book that just shot into the *New York Times'* best-sellers list – with a bullet.

Rosamunde Pilcher was home alone in Scotland when she heard the news. She celebrated with a glass of Famous Grouse, with ice, and "the doggies".

The German Connection

I should say something at this point about the incredible success Rosamunde Pilcher has had in Germany and Switzerland. She is a household name over there, not so much because of the novels, but because of the enormous following for the German-made TV films based "loosely" on her works – The Sunday Pilcher Special.

Our German-speaking friends have taken our author, or perhaps, more exactly, Rosamunde Pilcher's Cornwall, to their hearts. They have even Germanicised the pronounciation of her name, to the extent that it is barely recognisable to a native speaker: "Rozamoonday Pilha" – the second syllable of the surname a vigorous rasping sound, a more powerful sibling of the -ch in lo*ch*, as might be pronounced by some ruddy-faced fisherman on a windy waterfront north of the border.[2]

The first film, *The Day of the Storm*, aired in 1993 and over 8 million viewers sat down to watch. More than one-hundred-and-counting films later, the phenomenon continues. A new publishing expression has even been brought forth: Liebe und Landscahft (love and landscape). Today, two thirds of all foreign visitors to Cornwall are German-speaking. Upwards of 200,000 flock to the county each year in pursuit of images of romantic cliff-tops populated by well-heeled, gently-spoken English gentry.[3]

I would hazard a guess that Cornish hoteliers, letting companies, shop–keepers and restaurants have rather a soft spot for Mrs Pilcher. Tourism accounts for over 20% of Cornwall's income and in the 1990s the business was in the doldrums. Since then, things have been turned around, with lots of niche-markets opening up, a substantial slice of which is the Pilcher holiday. So much so that, in 2002, Rosamunde Pilcher was awarded (with just eine kleine Hilfe from Dr Claus Beling, the director of her TV films in Germany) the British Tourism Award for the incredibly positive effect that her novels, and his films, have had on the industry.[4]

4

TALLAND HOUSE AND VIRGINIA WOOLF

Talland House

There are three photos that caught my attention in *The World of Rosamunde Pilcher*, a book of her life in pictures. The first shows the house that Graham Pilcher's grandmother, Florence, lived in in St Ives with her second husband, the painter Thomas Millie Dow. It's called Talland House. The second is Florence in India with her first husband, Robert Pilcher, and their children, Hope and Elsie. The third has their Italian servant laying the table in the back garden of Talland and adds that this was once the summer home of Virginia Woolf.

Porthminster Beach 1918

(Above) Porthminster Beach 1913

(Below) Godrevy Lighthouse

Google tells me the house is still there and, true enough, for many years it was the summer residence of the Stephen family and their daughter Virginia.

I find *Moments of Being*, a collection of autobiographical memories by Woolf, though not published in her life-time. The essay *A Sketch of the Past* starts with the first, and most important, of all her memories. It is August 1890 and in a Proustian bed-time moment, she's lying half-asleep, half-awake in the nursery at St Ives, listening to the waves breaking and receding on Porthminster Beach below.

Next is a memory in the hall of the house – it was here that she was touched inappropriately by her half-brother Gerald Duckworth (he was about sixteen-years-old at the time).

Then there are recollections of digging in the sand, clambering over rocks, finding anemones and small fish trapped in rock pools. Her conclusion – summer in St Ives was the best imaginable beginning to a life.

There's also a description of St Ives in the 1880s – a pyramid of granite houses washed with a colour akin to her favourite cream, huddling in the hollow under The Island. Houses with thick, granite-block walls with stairs running up from the pavement to the door. A windy, noisy, fishy, vociferous, narrow-streeted town, looking like a bunch of rough mussels or oysters all crowded together on a rock.

The Stephen family would rent Talland House every summer from 1882 to 1894. The garden ran off down the hill in a series of little lawns surrounded by thick escallonia bushes. The great scoop of the sea was always changing colour: deep blue, emerald, green, purple, silver. And it had a perfect view across the bay to Godrevy Lighthouse.

At the end of the summer of 1894, a "For Sale" board appears on the grassy mound in the garden (the summer transfer was becoming too much of a burden on the household) and she realises that the paradisiacal period might be coming to an end. On top of this, her mother dies suddenly in May of the following year. Her mother's death, concomitant with her expulsion from this Cornish Eden, provided the underlying impetus for her masterpiece, *To the Lighthouse*, written some thirty years later in 1927.

A gentleman called Millie Dow eventually bought the lease and with that, as she writes, "St Ives vanished for ever".

We drive out in the direction of Carbis Bay, up past Malakoff Square. Shortly after, a road on the right leads to the lower entrance to the house, which is locked. We eventually discover the main entrance down a small side road. The house is still there but hemmed in by holiday flat developments.

(Right) Peacock-coloured sea

Talland House

Reticently, I walk round to the front. A sunny afternoon is drawing to a close, and two women, armed with hosepipes, are watering the garden. They are most friendly, obviously used to the odd intrusion by a literary pilgrim. They have no objection to my walking down to the bottom of the garden to take a few photos. They are, of course, aware of the connection (every time a flat comes on the market this is emphasised above all else) and the younger woman with blond hair tells me that the occasional visit by a like-minded spirit is nothing compared with the privilege of living in the house where Virginia Woolf lived.

The view of the lighthouse is now obscured but it was already during Woolf's tenure, her mother being most annoyed by the great, square, oat-cake coloured hotel that took its place.

The new purchaser, Thomas Millie Dow, was born on 28 October 1848 at Dysart in Fife. Expected to join the family law firm, Dow had other plans, enrolling himself at art school in Paris.

When he returned, Thomas, in his early thirties, started walking out with a certain Florence Cox. The Cox family, seeing the romance progressing, decided to put an end to their daughter's relationship with the penniless artist. Their decision was to ship her out to India with the "fishing fleet" (thus called because the women were sent out "to angle" for a husband).

And, in India, she did in fact meet and marry a Colonial Officer, Robert Pilcher. They had two children, a daughter, Elsie and a son, Hope. Shortly after her son's birth her husband died of repetitive fever and she returned to Scotland. There she met up again with Thomas who, despite travelling the world, had stayed constant to his former sweetheart. The couple married in 1891 and their daughter, Mary Rosamunde, arrived the following year. Cornwall was chosen because of his bad health and St Ives, I imagine, because word was spreading of the burgeoning artistic community in the town.

Virginia Woolf kept in touch, returning to Carbis Bay in 1905 and taking tea with the Dows at Talland.

Hope Pilcher had a son called Graham, who, at Talland House in 1946, met a Wren who had just finished her service in Trincomallee (in latter-day Ceylon) called Rosamunde Scott. The reason why Graham Pilcher, commander of a Black Watch battalion, troop-trainer for the D-Day landings, decorated by Montgomery, was staying with his grandmother at Talland was because, in October 1944, he had been seriously injured fighting south of Bremen in the final push towards Germany. The surgeon who operated on him in the field said that he had never given anyone so much blood in the whole of his professional career. The young couple (she was twenty-two, he was thirty) would go on to marry in St Uny church in Lelant on 7 December 1946. Witnesses were her father and Florence Dow.

A rather long-winded preamble to get to the point, I hear you muttering. The method behind my madness is that I am convinced that Talland House is, in more senses than one, the place which got Rosamunde Pilcher the novelist started.

I am sure that she would have gone on to write without the Talland connection. Nevertheless, I would be surprised if she wasn't inspired to some extent by her fiancé's grandmother's stories about Woolf, the house and the lighthouse.

The story of Thomas waiting for Florence for so many years, meeting up again and marrying – did that provide a seed for the theme of searching for past loves that crops up so often in her work?

Rosamunde Pilcher's marriage certificate

Next, there's Millie Dow, the penniless artist, who goes on, in fact, to become a nationally well-known, well-respected and admired painter – President of the St Ives Society of Artists, one of the Glasgow Boys School. Isn't it likely that that's where another recurring Pilcher motif – that a painting hanging on a wall in your house could possibly be worth a fortune – had its roots?

To finish, a titbit for lovers of *The Antiques Roadshow* like myself. If you do happen to have a Millie Dow over the fireplace in the front room, I'm afraid it's not going to be worth as much as the painting *The Shell Seekers*. However, a small watercolour from 1885 entitled *White Roses in a Blue Vase* was sold at Bonham's in 2017 for 8,360 euros – so certainly not to be sniffed at.

Tregenna Castle

Just up the road from Talland House is the entrance to Tregenna Castle. It's an 84-bedroomed hotel, set in enormous grounds (72 acres) given over to lawns and terraces with panoramic views over the bay, tennis courts and above all an 18-hole golf-course.

It was built for Samuel Stephens in 1774. Stephens, Mayor and incoming reformer, was much involved in the transformation in character and wealth that the town underwent at this time. In the process he also transformed himself, from merchant to gentleman to Member of Parliament.

Tregenna Castle

Godrevy Lighthouse (seen from the 7th hole)

The GWR bought Tregenna as a hotel in 1878. As the guide points out, the east entrance front, though much altered and extended, is more or less original, but very little else is, inside or out. This is where Lesley Stephen stayed on his first visit to St Ives on his search for a summer home.

Tregenna, in the Pilcher oeuvre, usually goes by the name of the Castle Hotel. One gets the feeling that the younger, more conventional Pilcher was quite impressed by the place, as it is always the hotel where the young heroines are taken when they need, in turn, to be impressed by the male character. It has fallen from favour by the time of *The Shell Seekers*.

Porthminster Beach

Porthminster is the beach below Talland House where Virginia Woolf and her siblings would have played. It is still the main family beach in St Ives, not having the waves, wetsuits and surfboards of Porthmeor. The walk up across and down from the town past Pedn Olva, or across the sands at low tide, is always pleasant.

Porthminster Beach seen from Smeaton's Pier

We start from the harbour. Just past the church, a small crowd has gathered, leaning over the railings, looking onto a scrap of black beach, or rather boulders. It turns out a stone-stacker is at work, swiftly and deftly creating gravity- and balance-defying columns made up of rocks standing on their ends. It's the first time I have come across the art (sport?) but apparently there is even a European Stacking Championship. The activity on this pretty redundant triangle of beach seems quite innocuous and the crowd love it. However, the stackers also have a predilection for pre-historic sites, important precisely because of the configuration of their stones. When you start to dismantle ancient cairns just to get views on instagram, then you can see why it has started to worry the heritage experts.

A stone-stacker at work

Pedn Olva point and hotel

Approaching Porthminster Beach

Where the path levels out and starts to descend towards Porthminster Beach, stands the Pedn Olva (Look-out on the Headland) Hotel. In the eighteenth century, the engine house of a copper mine stood here, the adit of which was driven westwards under the town for a distance of 95 metres. By the 1860s the mining company had already run out of money. Industrial remains can still be seen at low tide at the foot of the hotel. The staircase of the engine house was incorporated into the building. The path to the sands runs down past gardens with red-hot pokers, palms and silver-green spear-like plants.

One evening, a couple of days into our stay, we have booked a table at the Porthminster Beach Café. We are sitting on the outdoors terrace, enjoying a perfectly cooked piece of hake, with manchego sauce, saffron potatoes, samphire and clams. As darkness falls, the lights of fishing boats appear, strung out in a line just off-shore. After a couple of sunny but hazy days, I realise that the stars are now visible. And no, it's not my imagination – there, in the black where the horizon must be, I finally get to see the light from the Godrevy Lighthouse. A lonely flickering call for help.

Silver-green spear-like plants (Woolf)

(Left) Porthminster Beach Bar

St Ives town from Porthminster Beach

5
ST IVES – A NATURAL PHENOMENON

Porthgwidden Sands

The St Ives Effect

One morning, early, I go to get something from the car and stop to look over the wall onto Porthgwidden Sands. The sun is just coming up and I get to thinking. Why are the rocks surrounding the beach so black and yet the sand is such a golden colour? Wouldn't the sand be formed from the erosion of the cliffs?

And then – everyone says the light is so special here, why? And how can the sea be so many shades of blue and green? Basically, what is it that goes to make up that vision of St Ives that is so much admired and painted?

As a Virgo, not content with just experiencing and enjoying the wonderful views, I need to go off and do some research to find out just what is happening here.

Start with the light. It's the location. Like an ideal artist's studio, the town and especially the studios of Porthmeor Beach face north. Northern light is reflected light and has a constancy of quality – not so many shifting shadows – which is very conducive to painting.

Like Venice, the town, built as it is on the sand bar that joins the mainland to The Island, is effectively surrounded by water – again the light is being reflected upwards onto the houses and buildings from below in a perpetual shimmering effect.

The black rocks are volcanic in origin. Rapidly cooling magma has produced dark, almost black, very hard basaltic rocks, with a fine crystalline structure, known as gabbro and dolerite. The sea has, over time, then cut into the softer mudstones, sandstones and limestones of the bays, leaving the more resistant igneous cliffs, headlands and promontories jutting out into the sea. These now form the black frames to the beaches.

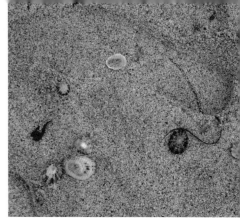

The sand on Porthmeor Beach

Black dolerite or gabbro rock

Xanthoria parietina

Apex predator

Warning sign

The sand. The sand at Porthmeor and Porthgwidden Beach is formed of up to 80% carbonate content. That is to say, it's composed of billions of tiny fragments of shells, reduced to grains by the pounding of the waves. Only 20% of its composition is down to erosion of the cliffs.

Here an interesting optical effect comes into play. Framing a bright colour with a dark contrasting one, say, for example, surrounding a red square with a black border, actually seems to make the red appear brighter. Gauguin, for instance, uses a black outline, a cloisonné effect, to make his yellows, pinks and reds stand out even more – they really ping off the canvas. The black cliffs make the yellow of the sands sing.

What's more, if you go right up close, sit down on the beach and scoop up a handful of sand, you will see that it's not just tiny yellow and white grains; there are many particles of black, too. The colour-enhancing process is also going on at a micro level.

It is the brilliance of this sand combined with the shallow waters of the bay that give the sea that whole range of blues, greens, and aquamarines, which in turn deepen and lighten as the shadows of the clouds scud across the skies.

The other highly striking feature that makes the place so photogenic are the roofs. The jumbled, pêle-mêle, abstract geometric patterns – a result of the irregular street layout in the old town – are reminiscent of certain paintings by Klee or Klimt. And all are dusted with that characteristic saffron-hue.

Xanthoria parietina. It's a family of lichens – xanthos means yellow or golden-haired in Greek – think carrot in Spanish – zanahoria.[5] Wikipedia explains that it goes under the name of common orange lichen, or maritime sunburst lichen. A very pollution tolerant species. Prefers growing on bark and wood – is this the right one? But here we go – nutrient enrichment by bird droppings enhances the ability of this species to grow on rock.

So don't be so hard on the gulls – the apex predators here – stealing as they do your pasties, chips, ice-cream or anything that looks vaguely edible that you might have in your hand at the time. Go lightly on them because without their considerable guano-producing capabilities (to receive a direct hit is of course lucky) a very important component would be missing from the colour palette of the St Ives we know today.

41

The quality of light in October

Pevsner chose Trevethey Quoit, near Liskeard, to grace the cover of his Cornwall Guide

The St Ives effect was what prompted Betjeman in his Shell Guide to write:

"Yet he who breasts the hill on the road from Hayle after the sprawling villadom of Carbis Bay, passing the landward leaning woods of Tregenna Castle… he who passes these things and gazes down on the huddled town on its promontory below him, can hardly restrain a gasp of admiration."

All the above was written in June. We return in October and the quality of light has gone up several notches (and it was impressive before.) On a bright windy autumn day, the air is crisper, the blue of the sky bluer. Even at midday (the worst time usually for taking photos) because the sun is not climbing so high in the sky, the shadows are deeper, longer and more defined. Everything stands out more: every line, every shape is just that bit more distinct. It is truly remarkable.

Our Guides

I should explain about the guidebooks. There is a fashion at the moment for using vintage guidebooks. BBC Radio 4 have recently been touring with the old Penguin guides, and you can turn on the TV almost any evening of the week and find a multi-coloured Michael Portillo bouncing along in a railway carriage, Bradshaw's Railway Guide in hand.

I, too, therefore, have found myself three mid-century guides to Cornwall: the Penguin, a Shell Guide (written by John Betjeman) and a Pevsner (Volume 1 of *The Buildings of England*).

The Penguin is quickly discarded – a lightweight, superficial booklet. The only thing I have noted down is an unfortunate error of punctuation, "The best known features of Cornish diet are pasties, pilchards and cream, and saffron cake". An unusual flavour combination.

Betjeman and Pevsner are more interesting.

Nikolaus Pevsner was born into a Russian-Jewish family in Leipzig in 1902. In 1933, he leaves Germany for England when Jews are no longer permitted to teach at the university (he was a lecturer in Art History).[6] It would take him a full twenty-six years (1948 to 1974) to catalogue and to describe, in 46 volumes, the whole of English architecture.

His main competitors, as he started out, were the Shell guides conceived in the early 1930s by John Betjeman. Like Betjeman, Pevsner started the series with Cornwall. His publisher, probably decided to go with the most commercially attractive volume first – Du Maurier's novels were highly popular at the time. There was also the irresistible challenge of going head-to-head with Betjeman in a battle for sales.[7]

And so, the famous feud between the two men takes off – fuelled more by Betjeman, perhaps, because he himself had intended to embark on a series of more architecturally focused guides at the end of the 1940s that never got going, perhaps because, by starting with Cornwall, Betjeman felt that Pevsner was simply treading on his patch.

Betjeman had always been quite scathing when it came to other people's guidebooks: "existing guides either give wide-angle views of public libraries or else they mention in detail what rent was paid to Hubert de Burg in 1186". For him, the writer's personal opinion and reaction were what counted – the eye and the heart were the key. Betjeman deplored the fact that, with his dry, academic style, concentrating solely on buildings, Pevsner was – in his mind – draining the life-blood, the soul, out of Merry England. Herr Professor-Doktor, he called him.

Pevsner, in reply, could bring up Betjeman's time as an undergraduate at Oxford (he failed to complete his degree, whereas Pevsner held professorships at both Oxford and Cambridge).

But then the two men's personalities were so different that their works were always going to be poles apart. Betjeman: emotional, intuitive, lyrical and all-embracing; Pevsner: concentrated on his subject, formal, punctilious, scholarly, analytic and disciplined. Just as Pevsner didn't write poems, Betjeman could never have produced *The Buildings of England*.

Anyway, in spring 1948, there they are driving off down the A30 – Lola (Pevsner's wife) at the wheel of their Austin 10 and Pevsner taking notes. Lola did the driving, made the sandwiches and planned the itinerary while he wrote.

Late of an afternoon, he would stop, reach into his pocket and take out a cigarette. For Lola, that was the signal that work was over for the day.

St Ia and St Nicholas

Rachel's absolutely fabulous favourite

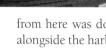
An "ope"

St Ives, The Harbour

The church of St Ia was built between 1410 and 1434. We know this because a Papal Bull, granted in 1410, allowed construction to go ahead. The church contains a *Madonna and Child* by Barbara Hepworth, sculpted in memory of her son killed on RAF service in 1953, which I've always wanted to see. Unfortunately, I have never ever found the church open, until that is, we visit this October. As we drive onto the Wharf, I notice people going in. We immediately park up and rush straight back round the harbour. Only to find it has closed once again.

Just up from the church on the left is Boots, the chemist. Take a look up at the front of the building – this used to be the Scala Cinema. It's here in *Coming Home* that Judith Dunbar, hoping to see *Top Hat* with Fred Astaire and Ginger Rogers, is sexually assaulted by the paedophile Billy Fawcett.

If you venture down the narrow alley to the left of Boots you will come to the Guildhall, which also houses the information centre. Outside you can see another Hepworth statue, *Dual Form*. The little shop opposite is a fantastic place to find old postcards.

Fore Street, the main shopping street, was laid out in one go, in a remarkably early example of town planning, at more or less the same time as St Ia was built. For hundreds of years, the only access to the harbour from here was down narrow alleys – known as "opes" – which led onto the waterfront. The road alongside the harbour – the Wharf – wasn't built until 1922. Before that, the sand used to come right up to the houses and buildings. On a blustery day in October, with a cold east wind blowing and the

Seaside shopping

Primitive Methodist church

The drum kit and "altar" table

plucky little sanderlings already returned for the winter, you appreciate the foresight of those fifteenth-century developers as you walk sheltered down the main street.

I notice that the doors of the Primitive Methodist church are open. Curious, I pop inside.

Down on the right, two ladies are sat down having coffee and talking animatedly about a funeral the week before. "Is it OK if I take a couple of photos?" "Sure, go ahead", they reply, "Come and have a chat after if you want." I explain I'm in a bit of a rush, but thanks anyway "Would you like some bread?" I tell them I'm just going to have lunch, I'm afraid. But thanks again.

I haven't been here sixty seconds and I've already been offered company and sustenance. If you're going to set yourself up as a church, you can't do much better than that.

There is a plain wooden cross, decorated with paper hearts, flowers and butterflies in front of the altar – no, altar is too stuffy a word – it's a table, a simple table. And they don't have a statue by Hepworth but they do have a full drum kit up on the platform in front of a colourful sun-burst painting, probably by one of the congregation.

I say goodbye to the two ladies, who wish me a good day. I can see why the non–conformists won out round here. If I were ever to take up church-going, I think this would be a pretty good place to start.

Directly opposite the church, you can step back into the past, in search of lost cakes, at the corner shop of S.H. Ferrell & Son's, bakers and confectioners. The friendly lady serving graciously listens as I unburden childhood reminiscences regarding the white card boxes she is using to package my purchases and my wistful memories of rice paper. "One younger customer brought a macaroon back last week saying we had forgotten to take the paper off!", she tells me, before candidly remarking, in a broad Cornish accent, "you must be one of the tallest mens I've had in shop". Regarding the fare, I would single out as particularly delicious, the aforesaid macaroons, the plum crumble, the egg custards and, especially, the saffron buns.

We fall in with the advancing throng of bank-holiday day-trippers on their way towards The Sloop Inn. It's a little early, perhaps, but I am missing a photo of the inside. In the dark, low-ceilinged rooms, people come and go, talking of fishing trip numbers, half-lobsters and the traffic on the by-pass.

Two weather-beaten, seasoned regulars are ensconced in the corner of the snug, holding court. Along with the beer, the banter is flowing freely. One, commenting on events in the capital, adds that his grandmother used to say, "Nothing much good ever came from anywhere past Hayle Bar". Another customer is asked where he is from, "Up north", he answers. "Is that past the second roundabout?" comes back the reply.

The Sloop

Inside The Sloop

The oldest house in St Ives (behind The Sloop)

The Sloop Inn weather machine

The Sloop is ever present in Pilcher's books, going under different guises. It is The Sliding Tackle in *Another View*, becoming The Anchor in *The Day of the Storm*, The Ship Inn in *The Carousel* and reverting to The Sliding Tackle in *The Shell Seekers* and *Coming Home*. It is here that Judith Dunbar, sitting at the table under the tiny peep-hole window, is accosted by a very drunk and bitter Fawcett. Edward throws him out of the front door onto the cobbles, and throws his whisky in his face.

It was always popular with the artistic community who liked to drink with the fishermen, not least because of the extremely flexible opening hours that the landlords ran in order to cater for the working hours of the latter group.

Francis Bacon was also a habitué in the late 1950s during his brief spell in St Ives. Known at the pub for his biting, caustic but witty comments to other artists, he also was in a scuffle outside the pub with his then partner, Ronnie Belton, getting a tooth knocked out in the process. In fact, one of the reasons he returned abruptly to London was that he couldn't find a good dentist in the area who could fix it. Many canvases were left behind; one unfinished nude was actually cut in half by an Irish artist, Tony O'Malley, who used the backs for two of his own paintings, The halves recently made their way back together and were sold for £30,000.

There's always a good-natured crowd at The Sloop, sometimes in the summer a busker outside, and the local lager Korev is a particular favourite.

A fishy alley

Bethesda Place

Zion Community Church and Salubrious Place

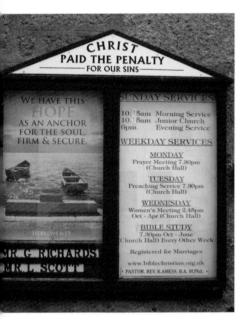

Bible Christian church

As you walk towards the pier, you'll notice that the streets and alleys on your left are never straight. This arrangement offers protection against the wind which is buffered at every turn. The houses huddle together like penguins for protection against the winter gales.

Street names are testament to the stamp that John Wesley put on the town: Bethesda Hill, Mount Zion, Teetotal Street, Virgin Street, Salubrious Place. Fishing families were mainly non-Anglican – Wesleyan Methodism was strong and there were Primitive Methodists and Bible Christians, too.

The disaffection with the Anglican Church was down to an ancient dispute over tithes levied by the church on fish landed in the harbour. Mariners' Church in Norway Square, up and behind The Sloop, was constructed in 1903–5 to provide an island of Anglican opposition in this sea of non-conformism. Small but lofty, it aimed to stand high above the scramble of fishing cottages and buildings.

Mariners' Church (on right)

No seagulls, please!

St Ives Society of Artists, Mariners' Church

The church was dedicated to St Nicholas, the patron saint of fishermen. Built to house 270, ominously only 100 turned up for the opening service.

In the previous twenty years, the mining industry had collapsed, the pilchards had disappeared: what were Cornish lads supposed to do, as the refrain goes? Doubt was starting to deepen as to whether a metaphysical entity could intercede in the slightest when it came to matters terrestrial. In short, faith was at a low ebb. By 1929 the church had been abandoned. It was never completed. The niches were never filled with saints, the bells never got their spire.

Yet amongst the ashes of this conflagration of hope, on this charred wasteland of lost illusions, artistic pinecones were already opening in the smoking embers, releasing their seeds into what would prove to be a remarkably fertile soil.

The St Ives Society of Artists were looking for a new venue where they could exhibit and, led by Borlase-Smart, in July 1945, they secured their first summer exhibition in the church. There is work of unusual design and medium by Ben Nicholson, with paintings by Lamorna Birch, Laura Knight and Stanhope-Forbes on show. The local paper also notes "Miss Barbara Hepworth has some fine sculptures".

Within four years, the more adventurous Crypt Group (they held their avant-garde exhibitions in the vaults below the church) had decided to form a break-away group and the Penwith Society of Arts was formed by Barbara Hepworth, Ben Nicholson, Peter Lanyon and Bernard Leach, Later they would be joined by Patrick Heron and Terry Frost.

On a Pilcher note, all this means that there is a slight anachronism in *The Shell Seekers* because Richard Lomax first meets Laurence Stern and Penelope here in 1943 – *before* its use had changed.

The church is still showing pictures of the St Ives Society of Artists today.

Mariners' Church, the nave

Mariners' Church, the altar
By kind permission of the St Ives Society of Artists and the artists and sculptors - David Moore, Seb West, Gareth Lye, Brian Busselle, Glyn Walton, Karen McEndo, Sean Taylor, Mary Ann Green, Ria Poole and Michael Chaikin.

6
WHAT ARE CORNISH BOYS TO DO?
1 – FISHING

Smeaton's Pier

The iconic pier that forms the outermost wall to the harbour at St Ives is known as Smeaton's Pier, as the first section of it was built by the famous physicist and engineer.

One of the main reasons for the pier was sand – too much of it. The same suspect had already spelt the demise of the port at Lelant. The northwest winds blew sand from Porthmeor which clogged up the whole stretch from the beach to The Sloop and into the harbour. As far back as 1538, John Leland was writing that "most part of the houses in the peninsula be sore oppressed or overcoverid with sandes". Luckily, seine fishing boats could still launch from the beaches and the late seventeenth century saw a boom in mining in West Penwith and so the town was able to survive.

The considerable expansion of the fishing fleet during the late eighteenth century, however, rendered the construction of a new pier a necessity. Work began in 1770 – the stone lighthouse, powered by gas from the new gasworks at Porthmeor, marks the end of this original pier. A period of prosperity followed. Main

Smeaton's Pier with seagull

imports were coal, salt from France for curing the catch, iron, timber and general provisions for the town. There was just one export: fish. Italy, above all Naples, was the top market for pilchards; herrings and mackerel went to Bristol and London. Associated trades were concentrated in the buildings around the harbour – fish processing and curing, but also boat, rope, net and sail-makers; barking houses[8] and coopering.

We did spot a seal in the end!

Plaque dedicated to Marine Commandos

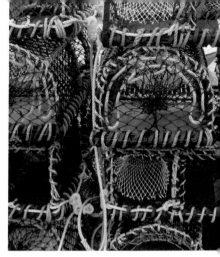

Lobster pots

Icing the bait

In 1888, work (commissioned by Mayor Knill) started on the extension to the original pier, doubling the length from 98 to 183 m. For this reason a new cast iron lighthouse was added. The three arches that you see beneath the beginning of the pier were added, too, again to ease the build-up of sand in the harbour, allowing it to flow out into the sea. The plan worked too well – boats were also sucked out – which explains why the openings are now baulked with wood.

Walking onto the pier from the quay, the small building on your right is St Leonard's chapel – once for fishermen. The red van on your left is Linda's.

There are various signs and plaques – two of them relate to Seals.

The first refers to Halichoerus grypus – the grey seal, a frequent visitor. Large red letters warn not to approach or feed. There are none around today.

The second is dedicated to Army and Royal Navy Commandos, billeted here while training locally for the D-Day landings. In *The Shell Seekers*, Richard Lomax, the love of Penelope Keeling's life, is an American Major in charge of training these troops.

Further along, at the business end of the quay, there are lobster and crab pots stacked up; in a stone recess a set of scales for weighing the catch; and sheds for storage.

Three fisherman stand chatting next to a small crane. They are complaining about the quality of the St Ives crane compared to the one in Newlyn which is " half the size, and twice as good" and "the position of the remote is more useful, too" One of the men shovels ice onto plastic cases containing what I take to be the spoils of the latest outing. "What sort of fish do you catch?" I venture. "Rays, monks, turbots, crab and lobster" – high end products then for the local restaurants. "They are putting ice on the bait for tomorrow's baskets". Of course. Job done, the man in the yellow wellingtons sluices with water and brushes the granite loading area.

On another occasion, I spot the Harbour Master in his office and, hoping to get some nice shots of fish being unloaded, I ask if the catch is usually landed early in the morning as it is back in Brixham where I live. "It all depends very much on the tides" he replies, motioning with his head to the large expanse of firm, golden sand behind him which forms the harbour at this moment.

Silly question.

The Island

I go up to The Island very early the first morning after our arrival, just as the sun is coming up. A kestrel is hovering immobile high above the grass that slopes down to Porthgwidden. Eschewing the path, I find that when I get up to the chapel my shoes are totally soaked with dew.

Pendinas, as this craggy hill is called, is where St Ives all started. A small Iron-Age defensive fort was built on the top and the settlement grew out from here along the sand bar that joined it to the mainland, where Down'Long (Back Road and co.) stands today.

Leland records that in 1538 the headland was equipped with a "pharos for lighte for shippes sailing by night in these quarters", but no trace of it remains today.

St Nicholas' chapel does, however, now function as a day-mark. The chapel was all but demolished by the war office in 1904, but rebuilt by popular demand by Sir Edward Hain to commemorate the coronation of George V in 1911. The Hain Steamship Company had the largest tramp steamer fleet in the country at the time, transporting coal, timber – anything in fact that needed transporting – around our coastline. Proudly Cornish, all ships bore names beginning with "Tre-" and had black funnels with a white H painted on them – Virginia Woolf mentions them. The company was bought by P&O in 1917. The fleet certainly contributed to the world war efforts of the last century – 18 ships lost in the first and 28 (out of a total of 32) lost in the second. You can see the ship's bell of the last in the fleet, *Trewidden*, in St Ives museum.

The cross atop the chapel

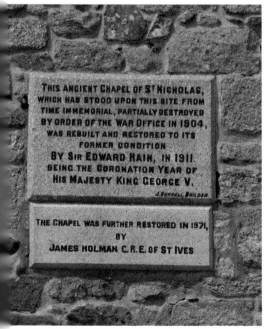

Details of the chapel restoration

St Nicholas' Chapel looking dramatic

Turner's view of the town from The Island

Pulling in the catch

The views over the town, and especially Porthmeor, from the chapel are spectacular. There is a sketch in the Tate National by J. M. W. Turner from this vantage point in 1811. Turner was the only well-known painter to venture down as far as St Ives before the arrival of the railway. His latest business project at the time, *Picturesque Views on the Southern Coast*, involved sketches being turned into engravings providing collectable and affordable prints for the larger audience.

I make my way down past the Coastguard Station and walk round The Island. Banks of pink thrift are everywhere. As you come to the end of the path, the extensively glazed flats ahead of you at the end of Porthmeor beach are pretty much where Laurence Stern's artist's studio would have stood in *The Shell Seekers*.

Banks of thrift on the cliffs

Porthminster Beach from The Island

The Pilchard Industry

Any talk of fishing pre-1920s in St Ives has just one protagonist – the pilchard. It's a small to medium-sized, elongated fish – usually caught when some 15 centimetres long – similar to a herring. Darker on top (olive greenish), its flanks are golden and the underbelly silver. There would seem to be some confusion between your Cornish pilchard and the continental sardine. The UK's Sea Fish Industry Authority in fact makes no distinction apart from age: a pilchard is a grown-up sardine. A look at the Latin name – Sardina Pilchardus – doesn't clear the matter up, but explains a lot.

The heyday for the industry, the absolute boom period, was from around 1750 to 1880. It seemed that the Catholic countries of Europe, especially Italy, Spain and Portugal, and especially during Lent, couldn't get enough of Cornish pilchards.

The fishing season ran from August till October. From 1829 to 1838 the yearly average export to the Mediterranean was 9000 hogsheads (casks). One hogshead contains approx. 2400 fish, so we are talking in the region of 21.6 million fish annually. As with most fishy stories, there are several claims as to the largest single catch of pilchards ever – the biggest I have come across so far is 57,000,000 (fifty seven million) caught at St Ives – in one outing.

To get an idea of what a Pilchard expedition would have been like, look at paintings by the Newlyn School. If you go for just one, then go for Percy Robert Craft's, *Tucking a School of Pilchards*.

Percy Robert Craft 1856-1935, Tucking a School of Pilchards, *1897,*
Oil on Canvas, 142 x 212 cm, Penlee House Gallery & Museum, Penzance

(Above) Sardina Pilchardus, 1877,
Les Poissons, Gervais et Boulart
(Public Domain, Wikipedia)

St Ives harbour with pilchard fishing boats on the left beyond the children

The St Ives fishing fleet in a postcard dated 1907

Sardines are still very popular in Spain!

The gulls have always been around

Fish Street

For a written account, perhaps the most arresting from the point of view of emotions aroused is Daphne du Maurier's recollection (in *Vanishing Cornwall*) of being woken one night, as a five-year-old, in Mullion, by her usually strait-laced Governess, who in an extraordinary frenzy of unbridled excitement, rushes her to the cliff's edge to see the pilchards come in.

The most detailed account is by Wilkie Collins, he of *The Moonstone* and *The Lady in White*, in his *Rambles beyond Railways* written in 1850.

A typical pilchard team had three boats including a seine boat (carrying the seine net) and two smaller boats. The seine was a fine-mesh net, up to 400 metres long. Buoyed up by cork floats along the top edge and weighed down by lead sinkers on the bottom, it would hang like a giant underwater curtain with a 20m drop encircling the hapless fish. The smaller boats carried another net – the tuck net – or sometimes just wicker baskets. These crews had the job of scooping up the captured fish.

The most important job of all (and consequently one of the best paid) fell to a man high up on the cliff. The Huer's first task was to spot when a large shoal was approaching. Huer comes from the French, meaning to sound an alarm. Once the dark shadow on the water is sighted, the shout of "Hevva hevva" goes up – "Found found". Then the look-out, a bush in each hand, waving left and right, up and down, would guide (like the marshaller who guides your plane onto the pier when you land) the boats into position. When the time is exactly right he gives the signal to shoot the seine and the boats enclose the whole shoal. The tuck boats now approach. The smaller net is dropped into the trapped shoal and by beating the water with oars the fish are frightened into it.

"The water boils and eddies; the "tuck" net rises to the surface, and one teeming, convulsed mass of shining, glancing, silvery scales; one compact crowd of tens of thousands of fish, each of which is madly endeavouring to escape, appears in an instant!" (Collins, *Rambles Beyond Railways*)

Then, quite suddenly, in the 1880s, the shoals stopped coming. Various theories were advanced: new steam-powered drifters stealing the catch, currents changing, water temperature rising or falling. Or perhaps just a case of colossal and reckless over-fishing.[9]

To bear this last hypothesis out, Virginia Woolf recalls returning to St Ives in 1905 and seeing the seine boats put to sea, something she had never witnessed in her childhood. 1905 is another year quoted for one of the biggest catches ever – 13 million. Clearly the lesson had not been learned.

But there is good news. The pilchard is making a come-back. Not as a humble, salty, fishy substitute for carne for our Catholic friends but starring in its own right at top-notch eateries such as Jamie Oliver's and Rick Stein's. The lowly pilchard – it's a sort of marine witness protection scheme – now has a new passport and travels under a new identity. Meet the Cornish Sardine.

Back Road East

Back Road

A left turn at the end of Wharf Road and then a left immediately again takes you to Back Road (note to drivers: these are the two narrowest and trickiest turns you will have to negotiate in the town) The eastern section of Back Road, where you are now, was the section of the isthmus up to The Island most involved with the processing of the pilchard catch – for these were the salting houses. Landed fish were immediately transferred here in baskets and barrows. As the industry expanded, the western end of Back Road backing onto Porthmeor Beach was developed with purpose-built salting-houses: quadrangular structures of granite, with roofs around the four sides supported by pillars and a central courtyard open to the sky – not unlike a Roman villa. They were known, in fact, as Pilchard Palaces.

The fish were gutted and then carefully placed in huge neat walls or baulks, sometimes one metre high by six long, made up of layer upon layer of alternating fish and salt. It was the work of the women and girls of the neighbourhood. Wages were three-pence an hour with a glass of brandy and a piece of bread and cheese

Horse and cart loading with fish in the harbour

The cottages have outside staircases

A fisherman's cottage

provided after every six hour stint. The fish would remain in baulk for five or six weeks, then they were washed and arranged in circular formation, tails at the centre, heads outwards, in large hogsheads. These were then pressed with weights to compress the volume for easier transportation, but also to release the valuable excess oil known as train oil.

For the visitor to St Ives in this period, the key word in the above paragraph is "gutted". The waste products: the innards, the entrails, the guts, are what W. G. Maton refers to in 1797: "the stench arising from the stores, and from the putrid 'rejectamenta' lying about the town, is to strangers almost intolerable".

I lived for a long time in Vicenza in the Veneto region of North East Italy. There was a town some 20 kilometres west of us, Arzignano, which was the centre of the leather industry, and had built its wealth on that. Due to various products used in the tanning process, the town was permanently enveloped in the most nauseating-smelling clouds. Just to pass through the town by train was unpleasant. The local dialect proudly referred to these malodiferous emanations as "La spusa dei schei" – the stink that money makes. Presumably the people of St Ives shared this opinion. The town thrived off, depended on, and stank of, pilchards.[10]

This also explains why the cottages here are built the way they are. The salt cellars were on the ground floors, the living spaces above. There was no way the staircase to the first floor could come up through the house – the rest of the house had to be hermetically sealed off from the work below. Hence all staircases had to ascend the outside of the building.

Norway Stores – Mr Penberth's grocery store

Inside Penwith Gallery © Penwith Galleries Ltd.
Magic Stone sculpture, Barbara Hepworth © Bowness

Further along the road, we come to a curious triangular-shaped corner grocery shop on the left. Norway Stores, established in 1896 is the oldest shop in St Ives. Based on the description in *The Shell Seekers* this can only be Mr Penberth's grocery store where Penelope during the war manages to buy crates of peaches washed up on North beach

A short way on again, we come to what is now the artist's half of Back Road. This is where the Pilchard Palaces used to be. A perfect example of what we were talking about before – the Roman Villa set-up – is afforded by entering the Penwith Gallery – home of the break-away Penwith

Foundation stone laid by Barbara Hepworth

An upstairs studio overlooking Porthmeor Beach

Society of Arts formed by Barbara Hepworth, Ben Nicolson and others in 1949. They moved to this location in 1961. The light softly diffusing down through the central aperture sets off wonderfully the exhibits below. One thing particularly strikes me: a foundation stone laid by Hepworth in 1973 – it's just propped up against the wall as you go in.

With hindsight, the fact that the rapid decline of the fishing industry coincided almost exactly with the arrival of the railway and artists from London was an enormous stroke of luck. The buildings along the right side of the street all back onto Porthminster beach – we shall see them from the sea side shortly. These were not houses but custom made fish-processing factories with ample cellars and also long, wide, lofty spaces above where nets could be dried, mended and barked. Before the introduction of synthetic yarn in the 1950s all nets were made of natural fibres – linen or hemp – and as such they needed constant maintenance. After his boat, nets were the biggest outlay facing a fisherman and barking was a process to counteract the rotting of the fibres that constant exposure to salt water would cause.

The fishermen had these vast lofts now lying idle; the artists were looking for light, airy, large studios where they could work on their canvases. Three other factors appealed to the arriving artists, too – the "studios" were cheap to rent; they faced north; and they were situated right on the very edge of the ocean, with a brilliant quality of light more often found in the Mediterranean than in England.

On a later visit, I realise I haven't got a photo of a studio. By chance, the door to Porthmeor Studios Art School is open, so I go in. An elderly gentleman carrying a box of fish and chips greets me. "Is it Ok to take a photo?" He has no objection, so I wander to the end of the corridor. The Borlase-Smart Room is locked and a photo through the glass of the door wouldn't come off. Turning round, I see my host has seen the problem. I tell him I don't want to disturb his lunch, but he tells me to come upstairs – there's a life class this morning, but they're on their break, so I can have a look in there.

The buildings have obviously been revamped: there's a lift and the old larger studios have been divided up to give more floor space. I apologise to the ladies waiting to resume their class, who, while I snap away, make themselves invisible behind paintings and easels. The slim, dark-haired model is over in the corner, in a pale lime-green bath-robe. I apologise to her too for the intrusion. Through the windows three bands of colour are visible – the sand (white), the sea (green through to grey blue) and the sky (pale blue).

The colours of the sea

The harbour on a rainy day

Doors

A Rainy Day

We do have one day of rain, which keeps us indoors for the morning. But it's a chance to catch up on some reading, refine the itinerary for the following days and generally take stock. And a moment to take a good look at the house.

The second-home in Cornwall is a sensitive issue at the moment, especially in towns like St Ives. In 2016, 83% of residents voted to ban second-home owners buying any new-build developments. According to 2015 figures, second homes account for 12% of all main-residence homes in the county. The main concern is that second homes are pushing prices out of the reach of locals – average house prices are running at £360,000 for 2018, well over 20 times the typical local salary, with Cornwall being one of the most deprived areas in Western Europe.

Cornish devolutionists argue that a local family living in the town would generate more money for the community than tourists coming in for short-lets. Yet, there is no getting away from the fact that tourism now forms the main industry here. Tourists need to stay somewhere, otherwise locals will find themselves out of a job.

Down where we are, right on the edge of the harbour, is an area which, eighty years ago, children would have been warned not to stray into, being the domain of rough, hard-working, hard-talking fishermen. Not so today – the vast majority of the cottages in this area now are holiday-lets. Ours is one-bedroomed, over two floors, and very nicely appointed. The colour palette is bare boards, white walls, pale blues and natural hessian. There are original art-works about the place, with your standard go-to Ben Nicholson poster – the one with the Union Jack, cups and harbour – in the kitchen. It has a nice feel to it – we even have a wicker heart suspended over the stairs. And wifi. Also, on arrival, there was that traditional Cornish welcoming present – the bottle of yellow label Campo Viejo Rioja.

My favourite thing is the front door. Ours and most of the other doors in the town are stable doors, or Dutch doors as they are also known. They are split in half horizontally, which means you can open the top half while leaving the bottom half shut. This has several advantages. First, it gives you an extra window letting more light into the cottage. Second, you can lean with your elbows on the edge and watch the world go by, or chat to neighbours without actually having to open your door inviting all and sundry inside. It is also great for keeping small children or dogs either in or out depending on the situation. And, as my Cornish colleague tells me, they are perfect for taking possession of your Amazon delivery when you are only half-dressed. Given the houses in the old part of the town are all of very similar appearance, with sandy-coloured granite without rendering, about the only way you can differentiate your house from another is by the door. Door-spotting becomes a new activity, and observing what is hung out to dry outside, provides a great way of working out what tourists get up to during their time in the town.

7

THE ST IVES SCHOOL OF ARTISTS

Alfred Wallis

In 1928, Christopher Wood and Ben Nicholson were walking along Back Road West from Porthmeor Beach. By chance, they glanced in through the open door of number 3. They saw a little old man, painting on the table of the downstairs room. Later, Wood would say he looked just like Cezanne. They went in and asked to see some of his work, and were astounded.

Alfred Wallis was born in Devonport in 1855. He went to sea at the age of nine. When he was twenty he married a woman twenty-one years older than him, who had already had 17 children of whom only five survived. She had two more children with him, who also died. By the end of the 1880s, he had given up on his career at sea and become a rag-and-bone man – his store can be seen in old photos on the quay side A WALLIS DEALER IN MARINE STORES with the N of IN written upside down. At that time he lived at 4, Bethesda Hill. With the decline of pilchard fishing, Wallis' business suffered, too and with his savings he moved to a cottage in Back Street Road. However, he had other strings to his bow: he could make ice-cream and thought nothing of wheeling his barrow to Penzance and back in a day.

In 1922, his wife, Susan, died and, left alone, he took up painting "for company". He painted on the walls of his rooms, on bits of cardboard or wood, or boxes – basically anything he could get his hands on. He painted sailing boats and nautical scenes from memory, in a primitive, naive, childlike way with no respect for perspective – usually making the most important thing in his mind the most prominent figure on the canvas. If the surface he was working on was irregular in shape then he painted his painting to fit in with the curves.

It was this natural, spontaneous way of working that the two artists, who had been approaching this style from an intellectual point of view, found so impressive.

As he grew older he could no longer take care of himself and he gradually became more difficult. He was taken to the workhouse in Madron, outside Penzance, where he died in 1942.

Through the 1930s, he regularly sent pictures and accompanying letters to Jim Ede, a curator at the Tate who lived at Kettle's Yard in Cambridge. I remember visiting at the end of the 1970s and falling in love with the house, its collections, its pebbles, the light – the whole atmosphere of the

Art is around every corner in St Ives

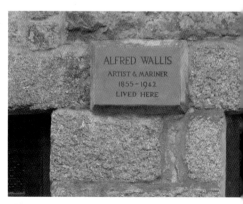

Alfred Wallis' Cottage, Back Road

59

place. And so many Wallises – there was even a Wallis on the wall of Ede's tiny loo, I recall – *Small Boat in a Rough Sea*.

I returned much later, in my forties, to see again in real life some of the paintings that I had by now in posters around the house. There was one I couldn't find – *The Blue Ship* – painted on yellow-brown grainy cardboard. I asked an attendant if it was no longer in the collection. She replied that it was but because they had so many pieces not all could be on show at the same time.

She told me to take a seat and disappeared. Five minutes later she returned and handed me the painting, adding, "Let me know when you have finished with it". Maybe they do that all the time, but I felt immensely privileged holding the work in my hands. It's one of the paintings where the space between the sails and the hull of the ship has been left unpainted. As Wallis wrote to Ede, "i thought it not nessery to paint it all round so I never Don it".[11]

The Blue Ship, *Alfred Wallis 1855-1942*
Photo © Tate, London

Porthmeor Beach and Studios

Turning the corner and walking a little way along the footpath above the beach, you can now look back over the wall at the line of studios. This wall was where it all started. Mayor Knill, at the same time as he was commissioning the harbour pier, also asked Smeaton to construct a tall wall along the length of the beach to halt the drifting sand that was choking up the town. There was just a small passage way down to the beach at the far end by The Island. Very soon the pilchard fisherman asked for permission to build processing plants abutting this wall. They had tanks on the lower levels for salting the fish and large lofts on the upper floors for the nets.

It is in converted net lofts like this that the St Ives School of Artists started – one of the first being Julius Olsson, famous for his large, atmospheric seascapes – moonlight was a preferred theme. The painters in St Ives painted mainly landscapes, (the Newlyn School was mainly figurative), and you can see how these early large expanses of sea, land and sky would naturally develop into the abstract approach of a Heron or a Frost. Artists such as Ben Nicholson, even Francis Bacon, for a short period, worked in these studios.

Lawrence Stern's studio, we are told in *The Shell Seekers*, is no more – demolished to make way for a block of flats. So this means it must have been at the far end of the beach from where we are now – in those glass-fronted flats which always make me think of goldfish bowls. This was the scene of Pilcher's perhaps only steamy love scene in her entire output, and even then it was probably more condensation from the studio's boiler than anything else. I say that in the nicest possible way – Pilcher herself bashfully but honestly admits that she can't do sex scenes, and confesses she much prefers "The bedroom door closed behind them, dot, dot, dot" approach.

Back Road Studios facing onto Porthmeor Beach

Back Road Studios facing onto Porthmeor Beach

Baywatch

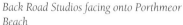

Summer surfing, west end of Porthmeor

In the mornings, we come for breakfast at the Porthmeor Café in front of The Tate and sit outside watching the day get underway with scrambled eggs and smoked salmon. Today, the sun, breaking through the clouds, is tracking like a spotlight across the headland and its World War Two gun emplacements. I hope to catch a photo during our stay of some latter-day shell seekers out hunting (*The Shell Seekers'* eponymous, and highly valuable, Laurence Stern painting is what causes all the inheritance squabbling in the book). The youngsters in the new millennium, however, seem far more interested in donning wet-suits and attending surfing lessons than looking for mussels, limpets and crab claws as we did back in my day – when such prized finds could be taken in to school and proudly exhibited on the Nature Table at the end of the holidays.

Today there is a good number of people out there on their boards – some more, some less proficient. I suppose the crests must be about a metre high.

Returning on a windy day in October, we really see what this sea can do. Over to the west of the beach, the waves breaking over the headland are enormous. Anyone out there today would be smashed to pieces in seconds. No wonder sailors and fisherman always talk of respect.

The surfing lesson

The Tate Gallery

The entrance to The Tate

Patrick Heron, Big Complex Diagonal with Emerald and Reds *(1972-1974)*

The Tate Gallery

If you continue on and around, you will find the Tate Gallery on your left. This gallery owes its existence to an exhibition, *St Ives 1939–64*, held at the Tate in London in the spring of 1985. After the event, Alan Bowness, the then Director (and also married to Ben Nicholson and Barbara Hepworth's daughter, Sarah), started to push the idea of a gallery in situ where these works could be seen.

Architects Evans and Shalev were commissioned to design a building on the site of the old gasworks, and apparently one of the remits was that it had in some way to incorporate the forms of the old gasometers. It does, although it has always struck me much more as resembling the lantern room of a huge lighthouse looking out onto Porthmeor Bay. A new award-winning exhibition space has just been added by digging into the cliff – this subterranean space being illuminated by a roof letting in sunlight whose beams hark back to the roofing of the old sail lofts on Back Road.

In the summer of 2018, there was a wonderful exhibition of Patrick Heron paintings. He is probably my favourite artist of all the St Ives School.

And there is always, from the café at the top of the building, the incomparable view out over the saffron-coloured roofs of the town towards Godrevy lighthouse – to be savoured over a cup of Earl Grey and a piece of orange polenta cake.

Barnoon Cemetery

One evening, having got ready early, I slip off along Back Road, past the Tate, and up into Barnoon Cemetery, to look for Alfred, who I know is there somewhere. It's far bigger than I expected. The place is empty – apart from the graves. There is a lower level and then steps leading up though a wall to a higher section. In the fading light, I turn on Google maps and a blue circle with an arrow appears marking my position. Wallis is up there.

It's then that I notice the man directly ahead of me sitting on the high wall, legs dangling. He looks Peruvian, skinny with long hair, a base-ball cap on the wrong way round, staring unblinkingly straight out to sea. I have to walk directly up towards him. At this juncture, two jackdaws decide to alight and hop from side to side of the path, criss-crossing each other, grave to grave, just a couple of paces ahead of me. I pass under the legs of our South-American friend whose gaze never wavers, and up the steps and to the right. All quite surreal.

Staring at the screen, soon the blue circle is super-imposed on top of the grave. I look up and I'm almost standing on top of it – its surface is tiled with a lighthouse picture courtesy of Bernard Leach. He faces out past the chapel and looks over to The Island and the sea.

At the funeral, the artist Adrian Stokes actually stopped proceedings as he realized that Wallis was about to be buried in a pauper's plot. This was one of Wallis's greatest fears during the latter part of his life and to prevent this happening he had saved up £20. A few days later a new grave had been dug and Wallis's last wish was satisfied.

(Below) View over Alfred Wallis towards the Island

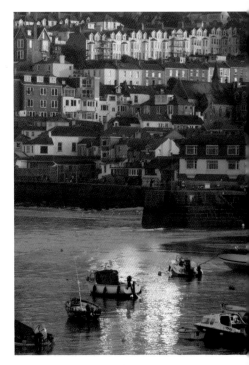

Evening reflections on the harbour

Alfred Wallis's grave

Hepworth's studio, as it was when she died © Bowness   *The Barbara Hepworth garden,* River Form *(1965)* © Bowness

The Barbara Hepworth House

For me, the high-point of a stay in St Ives is always a visit to the Barbara Hepworth studio. You leave the crowds on Fore Street, climb a small hill and find yourself in front of a granite and white-walled house. The formalities in the antechamber concluded, you go on up to the first floor. An art teacher is explaining to a group of students, their sketchpads at the ready, that the holes in the sculptures are just as integral a part of the work as the …

I head for the garden.

Stepping out is like stepping through into another world.

In the midst of cherry trees and bamboo, ferns and grasses, agaves and palms, stand the sculptures. The first on the left is a favourite – a huge elongated smooth pebble, with three holes passing outwards from a central hollow which always cradles a pool of water, and which has, today, floating petals. The central hole frames pink flowers.

Beyond the sloping lawn, and the wall painted light blue, there are the yellow roofs of the town, the expanse of the bay, of the same blue, and Woolf's Lighthouse in the distance

A lot has been written about her work. It doesn't seem to me very useful to analyse too deeply what these sculptures represent or mean; if anything words are a hindrance. Hepworth spoke on many occasions of her affinity with the Penwith landscape. She will have seen Men an Tol (see chapter 8). The sculptures here have a lot more to do with those bronze-age craftsmen's awe for their world than they do with loop quantum gravity theories and curved space-time.

I'll let Hepworth explain,

"The sculpture communicates an immediate sense of life – you can feel the pulse of it…. That has nothing to do with the question of perfection, or harmony, or purity, or escapism. It lies far deeper: it is the primitive instinct which allows man to live fully with all his perceptions active and alert, and in the calm acceptance of the balance of life and death."

The Ethos of Sculpture (in conversation with J.P. Hodin, 28 August 1959) © Bowness

*Looking out towards Godrevy
(between the chimney stacks),*
Sphere with Inner Form *(1963)*
© Bowness

65

One evening, after a day so long that Rachel is too tired to continue driving, I take the wheel, and, in the fading light – my driver now asleep beside me – we make our way across the moor from Zennor towards St Ives and out towards Carbis Bay to Longstone Cemetery.

It takes a while to find. Simple and understated, watched over by a sapling rowan, the head-stone stands surrounded by autumn leaves.

Hepworth's headstone in Longstone Cemetery

8

ZENNOR AND D. H. LAWRENCE

Zennor

We make our way along the road in front of the Tate and turn up the hill. On the corner on your left is the rather forlorn and neglected Holy Spring of St Ia, the town's patron saint.

The road then turns on to Higher Stennack Road. This was the road where the tinners had their houses (there were tin mines – St Ives Consols – just outside the town). On the left-hand corner, the honey-yellow granite building used to be a school, one side for girls one side for boys. This is the

The Holy Spring of St Ia

school from the opening scene of *Coming Home* where Judith Dunbar has just finished the last day of the Christmas term before moving on to the boarding school of St Ursula's in Penzance in the New Year.

We pass the Bernard Leach pottery on the left. The famous potter studied in Japan and on his return became a good friend of Hepworth and Nicholson, taking part in the first exhibitions of the crypt group and then joining the breakaway Penwith School of Art as one of its founding members. Unfortunately, the visit will have to wait for another time.

I am always surprised as to how the moor is there as soon as you leave St Ives. Ablaze with gorse, it's craggy and wild, just like Dartmoor. The hedgerows are high and are at their most exuberant (before the council steps in to give them their annual cut) with white cow parsley, red campion, hawthorn and blue bells. The road winds leisurely up and down as we track the deep blue of the Atlantic off to our right, past the stone walls of field layouts that have existed since pre-historic times.

*Higher Tregethern Farm where
Lawrence lived*

The moors outside St Ives

The deep blue of the Atlantic

On the crest of a hill overlooking the ocean, we pass Eagle's Nest, the former home of the artist Patrick Heron. Just a little further on, if you look back over your right shoulder, you'll see, nestling at the foot of the same hill, like a lookout surveying the sea, Higher Tregerthen farm, where D. H. Lawrence lived from March 1916 till he was asked, in no uncertain terms, to leave.

A little further on again is Tremedda Farm. Now, if you remember back to the chapter on Talland House and Florence Pilcher, you will recall that she had two children from her first marriage – a boy, Hope, and a girl, Elsie.

Hope moved back to Dundee to manage the family's jute mill, and had a son called Graham who later married Rosamunde Scott. Elsie stayed in Cornwall. She had a passion for animals (it turns out Talland House at the time had a cow, goats and ducks). She was determined to have a farm of her own. Her parents were completely against this idea, and incredibly, (given the experience her mother had had), decided to send her out to India for a year so she could forget her hare-brained project. She had inherited her mother's tenacity, however, and returned as resolute as ever on pursuing her dream. At which point, her parents relented and, her father having already acquired a couple of farms at Tremedda, decided to set his daughter up there.

The village of Zennor

The Tinners Arms

Wooden carving above the door

The courtyard of The Tinners

Her descendants are still there, having recently branched out into the ice-cream making business – they are the people who make Moomaid (mermaids have legendary connections with Zennor).

You spot Zennor church tower first and then a road turns off down to the right – the church and pub are in a sort of hollow. We park at the Tinners Arms and walk through to the main bar. I had seen the interior on an old postcard of the 1960s and it has hardly changed at all – probably not much even since David Herbert was here. I decide to try the Zennor lager. I can knowledgeably inform the landlord as to the picture of the ancient monument on the pump – the Trevethy Quoit – it's on the front of Pevsner's guide. We ask him to show us a room in the adjoining White House, having in mind to visit perhaps in the future, and I would love to get a look at the room where Lawrence actually stayed. In answer to my question, I get the reply, "He never actually stayed here – he just used it as a postal address". He goes on to tell us that a farmer who knew Lawrence has just died. The landlord went to school with the farmer's daughter and they still have in the family a lot of Lawrence's things – a writing desk, manuscripts and letters. This sounds pretty amazing but would, I suppose, fit in with the abrupt way in which Lawrence was forced to leave his cottage.

Lawrence and his German wife, Frieda Von Richthofen (a distant relation of the Red Baron), came to Zennor in spring 1916 and found a little cottage – Higher Tregerthen – to rent for £5 a year.

In March, in his letters, he is describing the primroses and violets, adding, "the gorse is sunshine itself". He writes of the infinite Atlantic – "all peacock-mingled colours" with the sea breaking on the black rocks of the cliffs. Cornwall is so peaceful and far from the world. The sun, the sea, and the light do his soul good and he has a sense of "a new spring coming very joyful from the unknown".

But, by 31 October (he has just finished the novel, *Women in Love*), his health is "miserable" – he is starting to feel the cold and damp of a Cornish autumn.

He does not become a conscientious objector but does object to not being able to express his opinions on the futility of war and the absurd loss of life and freedom it brings. He is called to Bodmin for the medical for National Service but is rejected on health reasons on three different occasions (he was to die of tuberculosis at the age of forty-four). What is amazing is that this man who was so sick for so much of his life could produce works which are so brimming over with vitality – I remember reading the uplifting *Fantasia on the Unconscious* when I was a student.

Presumably his opinions on the war were heard by people in the neighbourhood. There was talk, too, of his opening windows at night in order to signal to passing German submarines off the coast (more probably trying to get some air during a fit of coughing). He, Frieda and company are also surprised singing German songs at a Count House dinner at Carn Galver just along the coast. On 12 October 1917, the Police suddenly descend on the farm and issue them with a notice to leave Cornwall within two days.

(Above and left) Inside the Tinners

(Right) The Tinners Arms 1960

In memory of one of the last Cornish speakers

Thomas Millie Dow's cross in the churchyard

The mermaid pew

It is well-known that his experiences in Cornwall are recorded in the novel *Kangaroo* through his alter-ego Somers. What is not so well-known is that he wrote a short story, *Samson and Delilah*, which is set at the Tinner's Arms. One night, a miner, who had left his wife and child to try his luck in America, returns after fifteen years away. He walks up the Penwith coast, past the disused mine workings, to Zennor. The wife, the landlady of the pub, does not recognise him at first. At the end of the story, he reveals that he has saved 1000 pounds while he was away – a tidy fortune. A pint of ale at that time cost 3d, so that's 80 pints to the pound. £1000, therefore, would have bought you 80,000 pints. At today's prices that's the equivalent of £250,000.

The other reason we are at Zennor is to find Thomas Millie Dow's grave in the churchyard. After searching for a good thirty minutes we have drawn a blank. Rachel has the bright idea of seeing if there is a map of the burial plots in the church itself. There is, and we have soon found him. The cross – he is buried with Florence who died in 1952 – is the last before the stone wall of the graveyard, and faces out, his view unobstructed, over the moor towards a distant tor. Just nearby is a shining piece of black granite, the headstone of Patrick Heron.

Birds of a feather.

St Senara has a plaque outside the door in memory of the last person to seriously speak Cornish. Also inside there is the mermaid pew – a reminder of a member of the choir who was spirited away by a siren.

We do come back to stay on another occasion and are given a room with a delightful little viewing balcony that overlooks the church. If D. H. Lawrence did stay here, he would have certainly passed a good night, as the bed, with its heavy crisp cotton sheets, and divine mattress, is the most comfortable we have slept in on our travels.

The path down to Bosigran

Bosigran main cliff

The sheer rock face

Bosigran

From Zennor, we take the road to the right towards Land's End.

The north side of Penwith is much bleaker than its southern counterpart. Dry-stone walls, wind-swept fields with cows, mining relics – a tough, harsh landscape. Birds of prey wheel over the tors. The cottages square up against the Atlantic gales like sumo wrestlers – squat, muscular, with low centres of gravity; huge granite lintels over their windows and doors.

After 5 kilometres there is a parking area at Carn Galver. Down at the cliffs here at Bosigran is where marines honed their climbing skills for the D-Day Landings – in real life and also under Major Richard Lomax's expert eye in *The Shell Seekers* (Boscarben Cliffs).

The path leads down past very docile cattle towards Porthmoina Cove. There is a stream running down the valley which would have powered the machinery at the old tin dressing works – it looks a little like a ruined chapel. The jagged dragon's back cliff to your left is Commando Ridge which Sherpa Tensing climbed bare foot back in 1963. The towering vertical wall of fractured granite to your right is the famous Bosigran Main Cliff. There are tiny figures at different stages of their ascent clinging to the sheer face, while 50 or more metres below them the waves crash and foam against the rocks.

I am always at a loss as to how people can find the nerve to do this sort of thing: my palms are sweating just taking the photo.

(Left) Carn Galver engine house

Men an Tol

On the other side of the road from the car park, it's possible to climb up onto the moor to see Men an Tol, an ancient stone monument. (Note to reader – for reasons that will become apparent, please read this section first before you decide to start out.) The photos show two standing stones with between them a round stone with a hole in the middle, like a mill-stone on its side. It certainly looks the most unusual site in my little book of Ancient Cornwall. Legend has it that passing through the hole is supposed to lead to wishes being granted.

I have decided to arm myself with an Ordnance Survey app in order to facilitate the search for the exact location. I also check with Google and read some visitor comments. I am, first of all, helpfully informed that the site is open twenty-four hours. One reviewer then tells us that Men an Tol is Cornish for stone with hole; another that several women desiring babies have come away with raised hopes. A fourth irritatedly warns potential visitors that the monument is to be found at TR20 8NU and not at TR20 8YX, the latter address being Bosigran Farm where they live.

I have identified that the quickest, most direct way to the stones is straight up the hillside and then right. My route takes us up a (semi-)dry stream course, clambering energetically from boulder to boulder.

After a couple of hundred metres, Rachel has had enough and I leave her on a stone stile chatting to a couple of cows. Ten minutes later, the slope levels out and bears off to the right, just as the blue dot indicating my position is showing on the app. Twenty minutes on again, and I am now in the middle of the moor, still following a path clearly trodden by fellow travellers through the bracken and gorse.

A fork in the paths – time to check the app again. No signal whatsoever – I hadn't thought of that. The sun has come out and I am starting to feel a little hot in the collar department. I decide to take a left towards an old mine chimney on the horizon (later I realise it's the Ding Dong Mine) sure that I will soon see the stones in the distance standing proud in one of the fields.

(Left) Striking out through the bracken towards Men an Tol

Sometime later there is still no sign of the stones. I stop and look round – I'm literally in the middle of nowhere. On closer inspection, it also becomes clear that the tracks in the mud that I have been following are not even human. They are enormous cloven hoof prints. Made by some huge even-toed ungulate of almost Baskervillian proportions. A gigantic bull.

A military jet screams overhead. Can Rachel have called out a search party already? This clearly is not the right way. I retrace my steps back to the fork and take the other track up the slope. The path soon starts to broaden and tidy itself up. In the field to the right, standing in a bright yellow field of rapeseed, I recognise Men Scryfa longstone, a Bronze Age stone, with a Latinised Cornish inscription, which is supposed to be very close to Men an Tol. And then there it is – there's even a sign in the wall at the side of the way indicating the passage through to the stones.

It's not as big as I had imagined – there were stories that you had to pass through the hole three times to be healed of all ills or something, but there would be no getting through that aperture.

There is an American couple already there, too, who ask if I can take a photo of them standing next to it. Have they had a long trek? No, just parked down the road and walked the half a mile on the flat up the track. The app's days are numbered.

I will have to go back the way I came, however, as I have left Rachel with the cows. I am annoyed now with prehistoric monuments in general and despite the Men Scryfa looking great in its sea of yellow, I petulantly refuse to take the photo (which I immediately regret when we are back down at the road again).

Rachel is still sitting on the stile, alone. Her companions had got bored in the end and wandered off.

Men an Tol with the Ding Dong Mine on the horizon

9
WHAT ARE CORNISH BOYS TO DO?
2 – MINING

Mining Country

Newcomen was born in Dartmouth, Devon

Whenever you think of Cornwall, you think of tin, yet, in fact, it was copper that was being mined here when the industry was at its height. Mining had started in the early 1700s, much aided by Newcomen's invention of the steam beam engine for pumping water out of the workings. Water was the main problem in Cornwall where many shafts were close to, if not under, the sea. The steam pumps were later refined by Watt and then Trevithick.

From 1750 to 1850 Cornwall's output dominated the world's copper markets. At its zenith, over 600 steam engines were working across the county.

Incredibly, just a decade later, newcomer Chile's production had already outstripped Cornwall's, prices plummeted and the industry crashed.

Fortunately, some of the mines had discovered cassiterite (tin ore) at deeper levels and so tin production came to the fore in the 1870s. The greater depth of the lodes, however, meant that the ore was less accessible, and more difficult and dangerous to mine.

The boom and bust cycle unfortunately wasn't over – new discoveries of tin in Australia, Bolivia and Malaya soon meant local mines were no longer viable. Ironically, at this point, what had hitherto been considered waste products of the main process now become the most profitable sectors of the business. Demand for arsenic, for example, had greatly increased in the intervening period, especially in the USA, as a component for weed-killers, insecticides and paints

Tens of thousands of miners were forced to emigrate – to Australia, Central and South America, Africa and Asia. Some, more far-sighted, had left before the slumps arrived, knowing that their hard-rock mining skills would be in demand the world over. Others left when there was simply no more work.

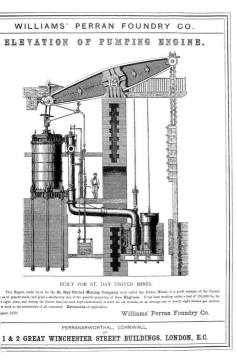

Cornish Pumping Engine 1870

Botallack

We continue southwards, passing the Geevor Mine (well worth a visit for mining enthusiasts). Our next stop is Botallack and the Crowns Mine Engine Houses – they're the ones down on the cliffs by the sea that you see in all the photos. The lower building pumped out the water, the higher provided the winding power to carry the miners up and down the Boscawen diagonal shaft in a wheeled box called a gig. The shaft ran over seven hundred metres out under the sea. Here, in 1863, the gig chain broke and eight men and a boy plunged down the shaft to their death.

Parked up, I scramble down, past the concrete dressing floors and arsenic works, to get my first glimpse of the mine.

There are 3 wow moments – sorry, I am going to call them that, because that is what I actually say – on our tour of Cornwall …and here comes the first. The sun is just breaking through the clouds, lighting up the engine houses. It's not just the incredible location of the buildings on the very edge of the ocean – it's the colours: the green grass dotted with white and yellow flowers; the aquamarine of the sea in the shallows turning to a deep black-blue over the rocks; the white fringe of the breaking waves at the foot of the cliffs and that thin line of white foam that serpents away towards the horizon. It is breathtaking.

The Geevor Mine

Mine workings on the cliff tops

Great for photos now in the sunshine, but a far from pleasant environment for the men who had to work here underground back then. The life of Cornish miners and their families was tough and dangerous. I say families because not just the men were involved. In 1839, more than 7000 children were employed in the industry. Boys were sent underground as soon as they were judged big and strong enough. Women and girls also took part, in the surface jobs – dressing the ore, for example. Children, because of their size, were also the best at sweeping arsenic from the calciner flues. (I appreciate that there is a lot of industry-specific vocabulary at this point, so I have provided a glossary at the back.)[12]

Health and safety was non-existent. One teaspoon of the arsenic produced here could kill six people. The way employers suggested dealing with this hazard was by covering exposed skin with clay and the mouth and nose with a rag.

Serious and fatal accidents were commonplace. As late as 1916, at the Levant Mine just along the road from here, the man engine, used for transporting miners up and down in the shafts, suffered a catastrophic failure and over 30 men hurtled to their death. The mine never reopened.

The Health of Towns Association report for 1841 showed that the average age of death in the Redruth district, the centre of Cornish mining, was twenty-eight years and four months.

The Crowns Mine Engine Houses

The manner in which work was distributed when it was available was also grossly unfair.

Basically, in systems known as "tut" and "tribute", miners were forced to bid against each other for the right to work, at "Dutch Auctions", which took place each month in front of the Count House.

With no prior knowledge of the conditions they would find below ground, miners were obliged to undercut each other's offers just to be able to put food on the table.

On top of this, they had to provide and maintain their own tools, pay for candles, pay for the processing of the ore, and blasting powder if necessary. All – yes, you've guessed – sold to them by the mine itself. What's more, they were not paid until the mine owner had been paid for the ore they had dug out, and that could often take in excess of two months. And, if at any point they broke their contracts, they were immediately blacklisted.

If all this was not enough, the whole situation was aggravated by the "cost-book" system run by the shareholders, the managers of the mine. This incredibly short-sighted approach was out to maximize profit as quickly as possible. The progress of the mines was reviewed every two months and if the mine was in profit then dividends were immediately declared and paid out – there was never a thought of long-term capital investment, or improving working conditions. Botallack Mine Count House, our National Trust booklet tells me, was the scene of lavish dinners when the shareholders gathered to examine the mine accounts. And on top of this whole pyramid of worker-exploitation sat the mine owners – the copper and tin magnates, the so-called mineral lords. Regardless of how a mine was performing, at the end of the year they took their agreed dues for the right to work their land. This could significantly reduce profits, or even turn a profit into a loss.

In this way, they financed the building of their sumptuous piles. A list of Cornwall's eighteenth century "fat cats" and their grand houses would include, amongst others: the Daniells (Trelissick), the Boscawens (Tregothnan), the Williams (Caerhays), the St Aubyns (St Michael's Mount), the Godolphins (Godolphin House) and the Bassets of Trehidy. This last family, who owned the mines of Cook's Kitchen and Dolcoath, were able to build their grand country house with the profits made in just one month during 1734 – £7040 – the equivalent of £1.5 million today.

Not surprisingly, given the extreme conditions and the hardship that the miners had to endure, they sought some sort of solace during their (often too brief) time on this earth. Methodism, with its central ideas of salvation in the next life for a life lived honestly in this, and its tenets of self-help, and help and education in the community, caught on quickly and soon over 60% of the population were converted. Huge crowds, thousands of people, would come out to hear John Wesley preach.

The Methodist Sunday school outing, a brief oasis of relaxation in this life of adversity, enjoyed enormous popularity in this period. Two humble but key components of those days out are still with us; they have also been exported, by Cousin Jack (the name given to miners who emigrated), all round the world and adopted and modified in their new countries – the pasty and the saffron bun.

Judith Dunbar, in *Coming Home*, also comes into contact with this harsh way of life. Here she travels to see Phyllis, who had been the cook at Riverside, and whose husband, Cyril, is a miner,

Looking southwards from Botallack

"Once through Pendeen, and past Geevor Mine, where poor Cyril was, at this moment, labouring deep underground, the country side abruptly changed, becoming bleak. Primeval; almost forbidding…The terrace of mining cottages, when she came upon it, stood isolated, reasonless, in the middle of nowhere. It resembled nothing so much as a row of upended bricks, cemented together and then dropped, haphazard, and abandoned where they had fallen… At the back of the wash-house was a half-glassed door, ill-fitting and the source of a sneaky draught. Through this could be seen a cement yard, a washing-line strung with blowing nappies and work-shirts, a rickety perambulator, and a sagging privy. This dismal spot was probably where Phyllis spent much of her time, lighting the fire under the boiler to deal with her family wash, or carrying a kettle of hot water through the range in order to wash a sinkful of dishes. Imagining the hard labour involved simply to deal with the ordinary chores of life caused Judith some distress. No wonder Phyllis looked so thin."

Coming Home, Rosamunde Pilcher. © Rosamunde Pilcher. Reproduced by permission of Hodder and Stoughton Limited

Dressing floors and chimney at Botallack

Cape Cornwall

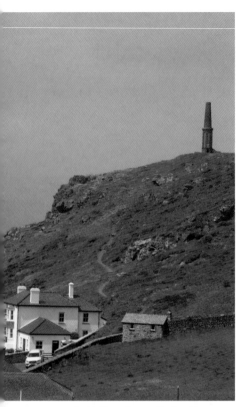

As we drive towards Cape Cornwall, white sea mist starts to drift across the fields and over the road, giving the whole landscape an eerie quality like a scene from *Jamaica Inn*. And then as soon as it had come, it lifts and we are back in the sunshine.

Members of the National Trust involved in Enterprise Neptune – the project launched in 1965 to save Britain's coastline from the ravages of ugly and ill-considered building projects, the dumping of rubbish and other forms of pollution – liked to call Cape Cornwall the connoisseur's Land's End, for reasons that will become apparent shortly.

The lady volunteer who welcomes us with the standard National Trust banter wrongly identifies us as from across the pond, a long way from home, and yes, we will definitely think about renewing our lapsed membership. An old couple in the car next to ours are peacefully, almost reverently (or is it resignedly), gazing out to sea as they eat their sandwiches. The views south towards Land's End and the views north towards Wheal Edward are magnificent.

I sit on a grassy tuft waiting for the mist to lift from the Brison Rocks a mile or so out. Two elderly ladies just across from me are reminiscing about playing in the rock pools in the Priest's Cove below when they were kids.

The Cape is one of only two capes (where two bodies of water meet) in the UK and until the first Ordnance Survey maps 200 years ago was considered the most westerly point of England. The chimney that surmounts the Cape dates from the 1850s and is the only trace of the mining that once went on at this spot after Captain Francis Oates decided to clear the place of memories on his return from South Africa. He had worked in the tin mines here from the age of twelve and later emigrated to find his fortune abroad. He rose to become Chairman of the mighty De Beers diamond company, no less. Arriving back in 1900, he built Porthledden House up on the hill behind you and promoted various schemes here – greenhouses, vineries – to give employment to ex-tinners.

(Left) Cape Cornwall, the chimney

(Right) Cape Cornwall, showing two chimneys

(Left) The Brison Rocks

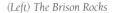

The curious ruin in the middle of the field is the medieval St Helen's Oratory, built on the site of a sixth-century Christian church. Rumour has it that the font in St Just's church is from here. We love Pevsner's comment on this – terse and unforgiving as usual: "Font – New. The date C14 cannot be accepted".

In 1987, the Cape Cornwall promontory was purchased by H. J. Heinz, USA, and donated to the nation, presumably in recognition of services towards baked beans by our compatriots. Figures I have from 2010 reveal what we have probably all already guessed – the UK puts away more of these orange beauties than the whole of the rest of the world combined: 1.5 million cans sold per day for an annual consumption of 445 million cans.

It would be interesting to find out what proportion of these are consumed in Full Englishes by people on holiday in Cornwall, letting their belts out as they relax and unwind.

(Left) St Helen's Oratory

(Right) Porthledden House

Land's End entrance building

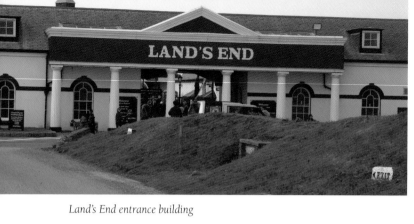

The First and Last House 1953

(Above) The First and Last House in England postcards

Land's End

I may have complained on occasions about the National Trust – let slip a comment about their volunteers' dials being permanently set to natter-mode; their continual checking as to if you want to become a member (are they all on commission?); the lack of wi-fi and/or card readers that means you pay for your parking with two brimming handfuls of 5p pieces gathered after 20 minutes of ferreting around under the seats of the car. But I had yet to visit Land's End.

As we approach the landmark, the First and Last motif is now appearing everywhere – the first and last pub, pasty outlet, beach…Our arrival is not auspicious. In the car park, we are flagged on past rows and rows of cars without a single space – I'm thinking airport long-stays before you fly.

Having paid our flat rate of six pounds, we fall in with the lines of tourists waiting to savour the Land's End "experience". The large white building which forms the entrance is a copy of the Falmouth Customs' House, by the way. I'm not sure *why* it is *here*, but that's what it is.

Back in the day, all that was here, apart from the rocks, the sea and the gulls, was the white-washed First and Last House in England, selling gifts, ices and postcards bearing the stamp: First

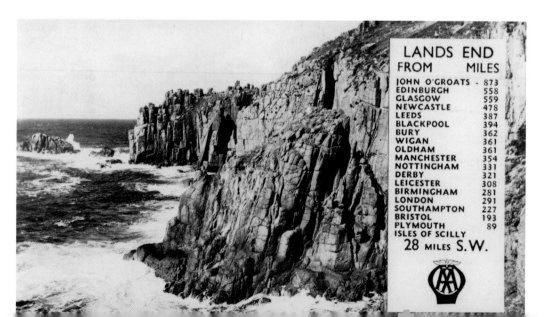

Land's End distances 1957

(Left) Rocks off Land's End and (Right) A stormy day in 1902

and Last House in England, because that was all there was. And, yes, there was The Penwith House Temperance Hotel established 1860 serving hot and cold luncheon daily (John Wesley used to come and preach here and clearly left his mark). But that was all. And it was still like this in a postcard I have postmarked 1956.

In 1975, when the book I am now reading was printed, it was still a family-owned property. In *Land's End – My Heritage* by Charles Neave–Hill, the latest in line, he states that his intentions are to preserve Land's End; keep it open to the public, as is right; make good the erosion caused by the millions of feet that have passed this way and keep future visitors to the paths so they will not dig up wild flowers or molest the birds.

However, he ominously warns that the Government's increasingly aggressive legislation towards private ownership, i.e. Capital Transfer Taxation, will bring the present situation, sooner or later, to a close. He adds, most hospitably, that most days he is to be found out on the cliffs and would be delighted to meet anyone who is visiting. Just so you can pick him out, his photo occupies the whole of the back cover. He stands windswept on the edge of the cliff, looking like a cross between Peter Cook and Christopher Lee in *The Wicker Man*. Behind him, being lashed by waves, is the Longships Lighthouse.

Our author was more prescient than he realized. In 1982, the landmark is duly sold, Mr Neave-Hill refusing the bid of £2,350,000 put in by the National Trust and opting to accept the extra £940,000 offered by David Goldstone, a former owner of Swansea and Cardiff City. A spokesman for the National Trust commented after the sale that their only concern was that it might be over-commercialized.

Goldstone did, to a certain extent, do just that, introducing a charge for visitors for the privilege. But it is maverick businessman Peter de Savary who buys it for £6.75 million in 1987 whom we have to thank for most of what we see today. De Savary claims to have had a sort of epiphany when his daughter was almost killed in a plane crash later that year, realizing that there can be only one point in making money: not to hang on to it, but to spend it. Unfortunately, good taste doesn't seem to have featured in the revelation.

Looking northwards from Land's End

Land's End 1973

A Grand Experience

New York next stop

Present owners, Heritage Great Britain, stepped in in the 1990s. It's a group of companies whose portfolio includes Land's End, John O'Groats and Mattel Play in Liverpool (an interactive family day-out featuring old friends such as Bob the Builder and Thomas the Tank Engine).

Which leads nicely back to what I have in front of me. Newly unveiled for this season is *A Grand Experience* – a chance to step inside Wallace and Gromit's Living Room or board a rocket with them to the moon. For those with a more cultural bent there a 3-D chance to experience Arthur's Quest and "experience the legend". Or buy a doughnut, or have your photo taken in a red phone-box. Or you can, just walk to the cliffs – they are still there, and it is still permitted.

Today the mist is coming and going in banks, and rock formations out at sea appear and disappear by turns. The whole spectral landscape is punctuated by the plaintive, mournful acoustic warning of the Longships Lighthouse, somewhere straight ahead.

There are several lighthouses round this treacherous stretch of coast. Longships lies about 1.25 miles from where we stand; Wolf Rock is 8 nautical miles to the south-west; the most distant is Bishop's Rock standing on a tiny island 28 miles due west of here. The infamous Seven Stones Reef lying in wait just beneath the surface is 15 miles west-north-west. This reef, on the other hand, has a lightship. Before you start, you can stop worrying what it must be like for the crew tethered out there in all weathers – since 1987 it is automated and unmanned.

The Seven Stones are linked to one of my most vivid memories from childhood. On 18 March 1967, *The Torrey Canyon*, a 300-metre-long tanker carrying over 100 million litres of crude oil, bound for a refinery in Wales ran aground here. For weeks, months, afterwards, on the news there were pictures of vets cleaning seagulls which had been mired in the slick. And they were the lucky ones – an estimated 30, 000 sea birds, gulls of all types, razorbills and guillemots were killed. You would find their mangled bedraggled black bodies in the thick black sludge that washed up on beaches all around the south west. The Navy was called in to bomb the wreck and set fire to the oil – 161 bombs, 1500 tons of napalm and 45,000 litres of kerosene being expended before she sank.

The official inquiry put the blame squarely at the door of the Ship's Master – he had decided to try a "short cut" in order to arrive more quickly at Milford Haven.

The last shipwreck here in 2003 was also caused, inadvertently this time, by the Chief Officer. He had, while on watch, got up and caught his trousers in the lever of his chair, falling and knocking himself unconscious. By the time he came round, it was too late, and the 90-m container ship, the RMS *Mulheim*, ploughed straight into the cliffs between Land's End and Sennen Cove.

Before we leave – we didn't stay long – I jot down one final observation: a difference between here and the National Trust locations we have visited. In the Trust-owned spots, people tend to take photos of what they are looking at. Here – I noticed it too in the Rijksmuseum in Amsterdam recently – the selfie reigns supreme: the image is worthless if the beaming face of the photographer is not occupying pride of place in front of the Rembrandt, or in this case, the wave-crashed cliffs at the end of the world, with, as a backdrop, the endless expanse of the Atlantic.

10

THE SOUTH COAST

Penzance

Tomorrow we visit Penzance. Pens Sans is Cornish for Holy Headland, presumably because of the passage of pilgrims through here in the middle ages. This part of the coast was known to the ancient world as far back as 300 BC as a tin-trading outpost. The coastal settlement eventually merged with a Saxon manor a few hundred metres inland to form the nucleus of the town we know today.

It's about 8 miles across the peninsula from St Ives. The road skirts the edge of Penwith Moor. On this road, at night, in one of the dips, Judith Dunbar's aunt in *Coming Home* smashes into an agricultural vehicle in what proves to be a fatal accident.

As we near our destination, the road curves to the right, and you get your first glimpse of St Michael's Mount to the left and the town in front of you. Arriving from the Land's End direction, the town presents itself in a very genteel way in a series of wide, leafy, regency-style Victorian avenues. Arriving from St Ives is a bit more lacklustre: a succession of roundabouts – the Cornish do love

(Left) St Michael's Mount from Penzance harbour

(Right) The Cornish Riviera Express steams into Penzance Station

The Humphry Davy statue

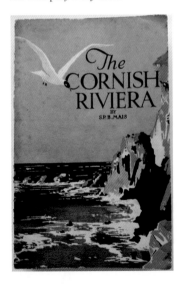

S. P. B. Mais The Cornish Riviera

them – and then you are driving alongside the railway line next to the sea with the train station visible in the distance. A poor cousin of the starting point at Paddington, it was once described as "a large dog's house of the nastiest and draughtiest kind".

There is still evidence of the sub-tropical flora – the towering spires of flowers emerging from palm-like fronds are, for example, Phormium Cookianum tricolor – the flora which had S. P. B. Mais waxing so lyrical in his landmark guide to the Cornish Riviera in the 1920s, and which featured so prominently in railway publicity posters of the time. The glamour, however – it is apparent already – has gone.

Market Jew Street's unusual name apparently derives from the Cornish, Marghas Yow, meaning Thursday Market. Postcards from the Victorian era show an elegant, bustling street full of local traders and shops – this would have, in the 1930s, probably been the street where Judith visits the outfitters to be measured for her uniform for St Ursula's boarding school and first catches sight of Loveday Carey-Lewis. The family-run shops have, as in so many towns, today made way for the large high-street retailers. Betjeman comments, "Since the war Penzance has done much to destroy its settled and attractive character. The older houses in the narrow centre round the Market Hall have been pulled down and third rate commercial 'contemporary' are turning it into a Slough".

The raised walkway is a pleasing feature though and the Lloyds Bank granite building at the top of the hill still rises impressively austere. In front, stands Penzance's most famous son, Humphry Davy, inventor of the Davy Lamp, amongst other things, which did so much towards providing light in the mines without danger of explosion. He, himself, modestly described his greatest discovery as being Michael Faraday.

From the port up through Chapel Street is the route taken by Spanish raiders in 1595 (presumably retribution for the defeat of the Invincible Armada) burning as they went all the buildings in the medieval town.

At the top of the street is the bizarre Egyptian House. In 1835, the then owner, John Lavin, an avid mineralogist and collector of antiquities, decided he would revamp his abode in the Pharaonic style that was all the vogue after Napoleon's campaign in the land of the pyramids. Opinion on his undertaking was mixed. Pevsner soberly notes its crazily consistent, if not correct, Egyptian style. Taken over by the

The Egyptian House

Landmark Trust in 1973, it is certainly one of the more unusual and flamboyant holiday lets on the market in the county.

Further down, The Union Hotel would seem to be the main contender for the Mitre pub that Judith is taken to by Edward after shopping for Christmas presents. As for the pub where Judith sits outside, that would seem to be The Dolphin at the end of the street or The Turk's Head. We snatch a bite to eat at the latter and I try a pint of the delicious Offshore lager, reminiscent of Amsterdam white beer.

On exiting you are faced by a Wesleyan chapel of cathedral-like proportions clearly placed strategically opposite this the oldest den of iniquity in the town. Built in 1814, the chapel had seating for 1800 followers. John Wesley, characteristically, described Penzance when he first arrived in 1744 as the place where Satan keeps his seat. Tenacious and charismatic as ever, he was able to say by 1780 that it was a pleasure to preach here. Almost seventy years after that, Penzance was still recorded as having 23 official public houses and an additional 19 beerhouses – one wonders what those figures would have been like had Wesley not showed up.

Cutting down behind the church, we arrive on the promenade with its impressive, gleaming white art-deco Jubilee Pool (1935) and its round-edged sister building, The Yacht Pub (1936).

Continuing along the seafront, just past elegant buildings which now house amusement arcades, we take a right looking for Penlee House. The house was built by the owners of the lucrative Vellanhoggan Flour Mills, the Branwells, better known today as cousins of the Brontë sisters of Haworth. Since their time, the house has been transformed into a museum and now holds the best collection of paintings of the Newlyn School – Stanhope Forbes et al. The tall 1000-year-old granite cross outside the entrance used to mark Penzance's central crossroads.

Further up again, on the hill, we have one of the main protagonists of the first part of *Coming Home*: St Ursula's Boarding School, which Judith Dunbar attended. In real life it was called St Clare's and is where Rosamunde Pilcher went to school from the age of eight years.

The Wesleyan chapel

The Yacht Inn

The Jubilee Pool

St Clare's from the side

Crossing into Newlyn

The house was originally built by William Edward Bolitho. The Bolithos – land, bank and mine-owners – had it pretty much covered. On his death in 1906, the house became a hotel, before eventually becoming the School of St Clare in 1917.

Its most prominent pupil during the late 1930s was the young Princess Aida Desta, grand-daughter of Hailie Sellassie, Emperor of Ethiopia, exiled by the Italian occupation of Mussolini and his fascist friends. During this period the Emperor's chauffeur-driven Rolls-Royce could be seen, on Speech Days and at start and finish of term, driving through the streets of the town. It may well be that the Princess, three years below Pilcher, helped to shape the idea for Judith's meeting with the well-heeled Loveday, although as we shall see, Pilcher almost certainly made closer-to-home friendships with other well-to-do pupils living in in the various manor houses dotted along the Penwith coastline.

St Clare's became the Bolitho School in 1995 when it went co-educational. In 2011, it was linked to a fraud by military personnel whose children were attending the school. An Army Colonel and a Royal Navy Lieutenant Commander were under investigation – accused of pocketing taxpayers' money paid in allowances by the government for military families' school fees. Fees which are to help, in theory, give their children an educational continuity as the parents move around the world for different postings. It may be that some similar form of educational or boarding school allowance was the reason why Rosamunde Pilcher, whose father was a Royal Navy Commander, and whose mother had, in her own words, to be very careful with her money, was able to be sent from Lelant to board in this exclusive school.

Not that the young Pilcher seemed to particularly want to go there, it must be said.

The school, which even as St Clare's had always had a somewhat chequered financial history, finally went into liquidation, closing its doors for the last time in 2017.

Newlyn

It's difficult to tell where Penzance ends and Newlyn begins for the new visitor. If you are concentrating on the annoying voice of your sat nav, it's easy to drive straight on out towards Porthcurno (today's final destination) without noticing it.

Newlyn, as one no-nonsense female hiking blogger puts it, "is a proper working port with no poncy airs and graces". It is still very much involved in the fishing industry as it always has been. It's up there in pole position for the UK as far as tons of fish landed annually goes, along with Brixham in Devon. Monkfish, hake and cuttlefish are the top three catches, with crabs and scallops both in the top ten. Cornish sardines just miss out at number 11 but are moving in the right direction from the previous year.

Newlyn harbour

Newlyn cottages

Just recently, however, Newlyn has made the headlines for another type of catch. Twice over the summer of 2018, the men of the Border Force have intercepted large quantities of modern contraband. On the first occasion, the yacht involved, the Netherlands-registered SY Marcia, was carrying a "cargo" of two tons of cocaine with a street value of well over £400 million. The two craft were tracked down and brought to bay, as it were, by an unlikely-and-slightly-comical-sounding task force, the mere mention of whose name must nevertheless strike fear into the hearts of would-be smugglers: the NDRT – the National Deep Rummage Team.

Before we leave Newlyn, here's a fact. It would appear that there is evidence that the ship, *The Mayflower*, carrying persecuted Puritans to a new life in America, pulled into port here to pick up supplies of fresh water, after judging that it hadn't been safe to do so in Plymouth which was in the grip of a cholera epidemic. Meaning that the Pilgrim Fathers actually finally set forth for the New World from the humble Newlyn, not the great Devon naval port.

Mousehole

NB – If you want to see paintings from the Newlyn School: Stanhope-Forbes and company, then it is the Penlee Museum in Penzance that you want, not the Newlyn Art Gallery.

Lamorna

We pass briefly through Mousehole and on to Lamorna. The fringes of the moor here are wooded, edged with flowers of pink, yellow, white and blue. The road turns left down a valley alongside a stream. It's like entering a primeval forest, shady and humid, with an abundant and riotous combination of oaks, sycamores, tree ferns and rhododendrons – the air is full of bird song. It reminds me of those National Trust gardens like Trebbah, for example. We pass a Victorian village hall on the left – a rather small place to find a hall like that – and other various expensive-looking properties: art studios and the like.

The cove, when we arrive, is as stark and bare as the approach was luxuriant, and practically deserted. A girl is, with a somewhat unenthusiastic air, opening up the café for business.

From the road into Lamorna Cove

At the Edge of the Cliff, 1917, oil on canvas, Dame Laura Knight

The coast path leaving the cove

My plan, today, is to recreate photographically, using Rachel as a model, the painting *At the Edge of the Cliff* by Laura Knight. It's the talismanic picture that Gus, the aspiring artist, carries a copy of, folded up, throughout the novel *Coming Home*.

Knight was one of the so-called Lamorna group of artists and was benevolently helped – he built her a hut to paint from – by the aptly-named local squire, Colonel Paynter. I know the location must be somewhere just to the west of here along the coast path.

I ask the proprietor of the café for information, and show him my photocopy of the painting. I get the feeling that in an instant he has mentally assessed my hiking expertise – large camera slung round neck, rather crack-pot photo-shoot idea, non-standard attire – and he tells me to be careful because the rocks will be slippery after the rain. I should get to Lamorna Point, but then not go down to the cross, just carry on. "Why shouldn't I go down to the cross?" I enquire. "That's why there's a cross," he replies.

My resolve not completely shaken, we make our way to the place where the coastal path leaves the cove. Three or four metres of climbing later, the resolve is fast dwindling. The huge boulders are greasy after the night's downfall and the path (if you can call it that) seems to lead off along the edge of a precipitous cliff. I have to make a call for the safety of the party and so reluctantly am forced to call off the expedition.

We retire to the café to regroup with a bacon sandwich. Several sets of walkers pass us on the way to the starting point, and also a guy in running kit, with bulging quads, who actually seems to be jogging the route. Will they, won't they be able to? They all return within fifteen minutes – except the runner.

Later that day, I do some research on the hall, the cove, and the cross.

The cross commemorates the place where David Wordsworth Watson fell to his death on 13 March, 1873. The twenty-three-year-old, Jesus College, Cambridge undergraduate was on holiday with his sisters from Northamptonshire. They had gone off to make sketches while he searched for ferns. When they returned, he had gone.

The granite waste tips that you can see on the east side of the cove are a reminder of the quarries working here up until 1911. They provided stone for many well-known locations including the London Embankment, New Scotland Yard and Wolf Rock Lighthouse.

The Village Hall only became one in the 1960s – before it was a Primary School (built in 1881) catering for up to 60 junior pupils. And that's the other surprising thing – the valley today with its handful of painter-residents and holiday cottage letters was once a thriving village community. Up until the 1950s there were far fewer trees, the valley sides being grazed by cows, horses and pigs. Early potatoes were grown and the area supplied Covent Garden with daffodils. The quarry would have been working and of course there would have been fishing.

Early postcard of Lamorna Cove

Dylan Thomas, the poet, stayed here between 1935 and 1937 with his wife-to-be, Caitlin. He described Oriental Cottage as "a borrowed cottage, with a jungle garden and three lavatories", and the cove as "full of good fishermen and indifferent visitors".

The cottage has recently been on the market for £675,000. And if you'd like the whole Cove, then that's up for sale, too, at a cool £2.65 million. For that, you get the beach, the slipway, car parks, a restaurant and gallery, two apartments and two houses, basically everything down-valley from The Wink public house.

The National Trust, which looks after most of the county's coastline, have said they have too much on their plate already to consider splashing out any more.

And as for the photo, well, I'll just have to try and come at it from another angle.

Porthcurno

The sat nav tells us that from Lamorna to Porthcurno, our next stop, is 6.5 miles and will take nineteen minutes. However, with the mini-heatwave that is now upon us every man and his dog has had the same idea – make for the beach.[13] Forty-five minutes later, we are totally grid-locked in a narrow and baking country lane. During our slow progress to this point, some indications as to the cause of the jam have become apparent: cars parked where they shouldn't be; drivers incapable of reversing; drivers refusing to reverse on principle; oversize vehicles that would not be out of place at a donk car convention. Cars scrape on roadside walls, people lean on their cars to get some air. Then someone seems to have worked out what to do and we start to move. 100 metres down the lane, we pass the main culprit, sheepishly ensconced in a slightly wider section of the lane: the Atlantic coaster, a double-decker bus.

We park in the extremely large car park near the Telegraph Museum and make towards the café. The baguettes will be fifty minutes, so Rachel decides to wait it out, people-watching, in the shade, while I take to the hill up to the Minack Theatre. Fifteen minutes later and mopping my brow I am buying my entrance ticket.

On the hill up to the Minack Theatre

The Minack is an open-air amphitheatre that has been carved into the cliff face. The audience look down onto a stage which is framed by the ocean, a breathtaking sight. Today an Italian tourist is giving an impromptu rendition of an aria down below us – a music student perhaps? He takes his applause and I start to look around me.

I've read that basking sharks can sometimes be seen from up here, and audiences, and actors, have been distracted in the past by the antics of schools of dolphins. The plants surrounding the seating are testament to the mildness of the climate: there are echiums, agave, aloe, aeonium, even bird of paradise plants.

What is amazing is that this is all the work of one woman, Rowena Cade, and her two assistants, Billy Rawlings and Charles Angrove. She had bought the whole headland for just £100 at the end of the First World War. Opening with a somewhat DIY performance of *The Tempest* in 1932 (lit by batteries and car headlights), she worked tirelessly all her life to improve and enhance the theatre, and was still working on it when she died in 1983 at the age of eighty-nine. Today it is in the top ten of heritage sites in England – I reckon many would put it at number one.

I should add that "carved into the cliff face" is not quite correct. That's the way it looks, in fact, but in reality almost all the components of the theatre are molded from concrete, using sand brought up from the beach. This enabled Rowena – who became quite a concrete expert – to carve the designs and wording that you can see into the still-wet seats and columns.

This summer the weather has been positively Mediterranean, but there will always be occasional hiccups. If rain is forecast, umbrellas are banned for reasons of visibility, so raincoats are a must. The show on at the moment is most appropriately *Tristan and Yseult*, but last week was *Dirty Rotten Scoundrels*, and next is *Pride and Prejudice* – so an eclectic programme for all tastes.

The Minack Theatre

Bird of paradise flowers

Porthcurno Beach

Over towards the left, there is a viewing platform that looks down onto Porthcurno Beach. There must be some 1000 people or more on the sands – that is approximately five hundred times more than there were at Lamorna this morning. The locals (and the tourists) complain about this overcrowding, aggravated this year by the spell of hot weather and the phenomenal increase in the number of people climbing on the Airbnb bandwagon. Fortunately it only affects certain locations – you need road access, a car park, and refreshments to attract a crowd of this size, so many places are still safe. Ironically, writers such as Du Maurier and Betjeman were warning years ago about the dangers of mass tourism. Ironically, because now outside Fowey you have a large sign welcoming literary tourists to the locations of *Rebecca* and *Cousin Rachel*. Similarly, Betjeman was writing for the Shell Guides, an idea to encourage the population to fill up the tank, get into their automobiles and visit all those far-flung unspoilt Cornish villages that the guide would, well, guide you to.

Guglielmo Marconi

A piece of ignorance on my part at this point leads to an interesting story which has proved to be serendipitously important for this book. I knew that from the 1870s Porthcurno had been selected as the starting point for a network of submarine telegraphic cables that united the corners of the Empire. For some reason I was under the misapprehension that Marconi was involved in all of this. Marconi, however, only joins the story at a much later stage.

He, in the meantime, has been working at the other end of Mount's Bay at a place called Poldhu, near Mullion, on the Lizard peninsula, pioneering the first wireless communication in the world, with the USA as a start out.

And, by 1927, wireless had taken so much business away from cable that the cable companies were staring liquidation in the face. In 1928, the British Government decide that they need to buy Marconi out, merging the two sectors in a new company called Imperial and International Communications Limited. Amongst other benefits, this brought Marconi enormous personal wealth.

What I had discovered by chance was that Marconi, whilst working and staying at Poldhu, had grown very fond of the young daughter of a local landowner – a retired colonel and the lord of the manor of a large estate just along the coast.

The flora at the theatre

By 1925, the relationship had been apparently going on for four years which meant that Marconi had first set eyes on Betty Paynter, a dark, lithe, energetic girl, Italian almost in appearance, when she was only fourteen. He then seems to have come up with a plan, strongly reminiscent of a Moliere comedy, to marry her when she came of age. He comes to visit, mooring his super-yacht, *Elettra*, just off the coast from her house. He even takes mother and daughter on it for a cruise in the Med.

All this is being followed at the time in the national press – the *Evening Standard* and the *Daily Express*. At Easter, there is a conjectured proposal on the day Betty turns eighteen and then just as quickly the engagement is off.

The stile

Cow or bull?!

Theories talk of the disparity of ages. Maybe it was easier for Marconi to bridge the Atlantic Ocean than it was to bridge the thirty-four-year age difference that separated him from his eighteen-year-old sweetheart.

By Thursday 18 April, just a few days later, Marconi is ill, clearly unsettled – "sconvolto" – by what has happened. He leaves by train for London, and yet Betty is there at Penzance Station as he boards the *Cornish Riviera Express*. If she had really broken off the engagement, would she have come to say her last goodbyes?

Her father, Colonel Paynter's irritation, on the other hand, knows no bounds. He issues a sharp order to the newspapers: "Please contradict statements in the press that my daughter, Betty Paynter, is engaged to Senator Marconi." When reporters turn up at the house, he drives them away with a horse-whip.

It was then that I came across a passage in Marconi's daughter's biography of her father. She recounts how he had (rather bizarrely) written to his ex-wife (her mother) announcing his imminent engagement to Betty. He tells how he cares for the girl a lot and she for him; he has struggled against the situation for a long time, but it's no use. And then, presumably to reassure her mother that their interests would not be jeopardized in the case of a marriage, he adds, "There would, of course, be no question of settlements from me or anything of that kind if I married her". His ex-wife is understandably first at a loss why she, of all people, should be consulted on such a matter and secondly upset as at the time of their divorce he claimed his family had for years impeded his work and yet here he was now talking of setting up another.

So was it perhaps that, with the marriage to his only daughter starting to become a concrete possibility, the Colonel got down to the nitty-gritty with Marconi and asked exactly what their nuptial contract would entail? If anything along the lines of Marconi's promise to his ex-wife in the letter had been touched on, that would have certainly sent the Colonel into a fury. The slight on his daughter's honour, the slur on the family name and the lack of money coming into the family's ailing coffers would have been unacceptable.

Ironically, it would seem that, in all of this, Marconi, a man who had such a great understanding of international communication on a scientific level and who had basically set the whole world talking to each other, had very little understanding of inter-personal communication with those close to him and just as little appreciation of the impact and effect that his words might have.

Penjizal aka …

Penjizal Cove clearly occupies a special place in Rosamunde Pilcher's heart. It first appears in *The Empty House*; is back in *The Carousel*; has a whole chapter to itself in *Voices in Summer*; and, of course, is the setting for one of the most poignant scenes in *The Shell Seekers* where Penelope vicariously enjoys watching the young couple Danus and Antonia together. It was one of her favourite places – but she had never managed to get here with love of her life Richard – theirs had been a war-time, winter love affair. Penelope also mentions that the first time she ever came there was at seven years old with her father. Was is that Rosamunde Pilcher also came here with her father on one of his rare trips back from the East?

And it's precious enough for her to want to put the reader off the scent by placing it on the north coast with the characters looking out on the blue Atlantic.

Penelope, remembering back to her childhood, tries to imagine how her father, the painter, would have captured the sea:

"For, although it was blue, it was a blue made up of a thousand different hues. Over sand, shallow and translucent, it was jade-green, streaked with aquamarine. Over rocks and sea-weed, it darkened to indigo. Far out, where a small fishing boat bucketed its way across the waves, it became a deep Prussian blue. There was little wind, but the ocean lived and breathed; swelled in from distant depths, formed waves. The sunlight, shining through these as they curved to break, transformed them to moving sculptures of green glass."

The Shell Seekers, Rosamunde Pilcher. © Rosamunde Pilcher. Reproduced by permission of Hodder and Stoughton Limited

The cove is a fair distance from the road, and it's a road where there are no car parks anyway. There are no refreshments and no toilets, so fortunately it's unlikely to get spoilt any time soon. But, this is where I get annoying – inspired by the novel, *The Beach*, I've decided that I am not going to tell you the real name, but keep it secret. All I will say is that, in Cornish, Penjizal rhymes with drizzle.

One of the ways you can get there is by walking the South West Coast Path. There is also another way that I will take you along today.

It's an unusual starting point. Rachel is sure we are trespassing, but I tell her no, this is the way I've been told. Sure enough, there is the stone stile. Then we skirt the edge of the field of cows (bulls?) that leads

(Above) The exchange library

(Left) Careful with that gorse!

to the farm. Just as in *Voices in Summer*, right on cue, the friendly farmer appears. There is even a little library in a shed where you can take and exchange books. We continue on a diagonal path across dusty, open fields now sown with low, green vegetables. There are fields of yellow flowers all around. A sky lark zig-zags off just above the ground ahead, flying with jerky movements, inviting me to follow her away from her nest.

Another stile and we are on a narrow track with hedgerows high on either side. The sun is directly overhead now and there are cabbage whites and 2 little brown butterflies dancing ahead of me. There is a buzz of flies and bees. I am getting hot. Quite ungentlemanly, but there is nothing else for it, I take off my shirt – if we meet fellow walkers I will just have to apologise for my inappropriate attire. The path eventually opens out, and we walk amongst gorse and foxgloves and yellow and blue flowers.

(Left) Almost there

(Right) Looking back in the direction of Land's End

Just as my companion is starting to give up on the guide, the cliffs come into sight and the path starts to curve, slowly descending to the left. There is a stream running down a small valley.

And then there it is. Wow #2.

A small group of people are sitting on the small scrap of beach just over the wooden bridge. We will not intrude – there isn't space at high tide anyway and the view perched way up here, on the side of the path, with the gorse and the butterflies, is amazing enough.

A final observation. *Winter Solstice*, Pilcher's last book, is set entirely in snow-covered Scotland, as a group of people make preparations for Christmas. But the author makes it so Elfrida, the main character, I can't remember now by what ruse or stratagem, has to visit just one other location in the 700 odd pages – Cornwall, it goes without saying, St Ives, always, and … Penjizal.

(Right) Wow #2

*Jade-green, streaked
with aquamarine*

11

THE LIZARD PENINSULA

The Lizard

Today our destination is the Lizard. The name most probably derives from the Cornish word for headland: Lezou. Apparently it's not down to the serpentine rock that forms a large part of the geology here. My favourite is that it's because the peninsula has more or less the shape of a flat-headed lizard – a Gila monster or some such. The road out of Helston weaves up and down, a tunnel of green, as we make towards the point. Then it flattens out into a wide expanse of heathland, scrub and gorse. It reminds me of Hardy's Egdon Heath outside Dorchester or perhaps a disused airfield.

And at that precise moment we pass the sign. Predannack Airfield. In the Second World War, Predannack was a base for Coastal Command whose Mosquitos and Bristol Beaufighters were ideally placed to patrol the Bay of Biscay looking for submarines as well as giving support to convoys entering and leaving the Channel.

The heath is here because of the underlying serpentine. When it eventually breaks down it forms a fine clay which, though high in magnesium, is low in nutrients. This is the perfect habitat for some of the rarest plants in the UK.

Although I probably wouldn't recognise them, the names alone of some of the plants are cause for marvel: black bog rush, bloody cranesbill, dropwort, night-flowering catchfly and thyme broomrape, to name but a few. The guide tells me that the best remaining areas of this unique habitat for flora and fauna are protected inside the base's perimeter fence. Only to then tell me that there is strictly no admittance. How does it go? "Full many a flower is born…" It is also one of the few places where the rare formicine ant (you will know it better as the narrow-headed ant) can be found.

I mention this because it is exactly this sort of insect life which thrives on close-cropped turf (the National Trust reintroduced grazing by cattle and sheep on the headlands for this very reason) that has attracted back the bird that is one of the symbols of Cornwall. It's even on the coat of arms. The Cornish call them Palores – diggers – because that's just what they do to find the bugs that they feed on.

Choughs (Pyrrhocorax pyrrhocorax) – striking birds with curved crimson-red bills and bright red feet – became extinct here in 1973, mainly due to loss of habitat. Luckily, three wild birds arrived back spontaneously from Ireland in 2001. And so far they have stayed. By 2015, there were seven breeding pairs.

A chough!!

The chough, in fact, is one of the main reasons for our visit today. Readers of my previous book on Daphne du Maurier (I hope you are both keeping well) may possibly recall my disappointment at not hearing, let alone seeing, the nightjar I was hoping to come across at Frenchman's Creek. This time I hope to find a chough, and if I do, I'll be well chuffed (yes, that is a pun, for those who aren't too sure about their avian pronunciation). The cliffs of Lizard Point are as good a place as you can get to see these very rare birds.

Mullion harbour

Mullion

Our first turn off is to Mullion. I'm curious to see the place where Daphne du Maurier came as a child. We probably don't stay long enough to do the place justice – we're on a tight schedule – but it's a bit disappointing. I can't see any trace of why S. P. B. Mais in his guide was prompted to compare it to Monte Carlo. The harbour is empty and deserted. I do remember a field of llamas as we drove in, but that's about all.

Kynance Cove

Kynance Cove is as busy as Mullion was empty. Even the National Trust website advises to arrive early to avoid disappointment. There are more than 200,000 visitors a year, and the cove has been attracting visitors since Victorian times.

Patronage by visitors from the highest echelons of society such as Lord Tennyson (who, in one of his more prosaic moments, pronounced, "I could have stayed here all day") and the ubiquitous Prince Albert, made sure the cove stayed at the top of the must-see list on the tour of Cornwall.

The Victorians were great lovers of outdoor living spaces and the names that have come down to us for the different features of the cove – the Drawing Room, the Parlour, the Ladies' Bathing Pool – are testimony to how perfect they thought this place was for their favourite open air pastime.

Mullion Cove 1932

(Below) Kynance Cove in 1904 and (Right) Kynance Cove as it is today

Carpobrotus edulis

Lizard Point, photographers on the right

(Right) Reptilian rocks

A picnic at the time of Mrs Beeton could be a lavish event. Ladies in their sun hats with long flowing dresses coming gingerly down the path, men skulking off for a furtive cigar behind a rocky outcrop, the domestics weighed down with hampers and provisions.

The Victorians, when it came to food, didn't recognise the word "restraint". As one recent commentator colourfully puts it, "picnics were extravagant, gut-busting affairs." The famous cookbook has a suggested bill of fare for a picnic for 40 persons. It includes joints of beef, lamb, fowls, ducks and ham; six lobsters, a calf's head as well as biscuits, cheese, assorted cakes and stewed fruit and, "not to be forgotten" three corkscrews – for you also need, for a proper do, sherry (six bottles), claret (another six), champagne (à discretion), two bottles of brandy, and three dozen bottles of ale. A final piece of advice from Mrs B. "Water can usually be obtained, so it is useless to take it."

We sit at the bottom of the path and watch a while. It certainly is a magnificent setting for a day at the beach and all the kids that pass us are off-the-scale with excitement and anticipation.

Lizard Point

Once arrived at the Lizard, we fall, not so unwilling victims, to the charm offensive that has been waged for days now, and renew our National Trust membership, getting a complimentary cold bag into the bargain.

We make our way down to the end of the headland where a small group of photographers – they seem to be professional wild-life spotters – have their unfeasibly large lenses trained on the water below. At this stage of the tide, the rocks, half-submerged off the point, are black and menacing like the serrated backs of gigantic marine reptiles lying in wait.

The walls that edge the path are smothered in the fascinating fleshy green fingers and bright pink flowers of Carpobrotus edulis, the Hottentot fig. This South African succulent is listed as being invasive. Here, it has invaded. I am musing on the plight of our native species when…

"Chough!" Not said over-loudly, but audibly – it's the man with the monster telephoto. We all scurry to his vantage point and there they are – a pair: hopping, diving and tumbling across the blanket of Carpobrotus that hangs like drapery down the cliff face. I include my photo as proof of sighting even if it is not the sharpest. The guy with the huge photographic appendage, on the other hand, can show off an image in which the individual scales of the chough's red claws are clearly visible.

The excitement over, we snatch a bite to eat in the café which is, it too, perched on the edge of nothing. Far below is the disused lifeboat station – the foundation plaque says 1914 – with its runway into the sea. Today the water is calm. There are three small boats fishing and the sea over the patches of sand is producing marvellous turquoise Patrick Heron shapes on its otherwise dark blue canvas.

We loop round towards the car park. The locals, so reliant on what they could scavenge from wrecks to supplement their harsh existence, were totally opposed to the lighthouse when it was erected in 1619. So extensive were the protests that is was closed and there was no more light here for another 150 years.

Nancherrow II

Our brief interlude on the peninsula is over and the search for Pilcher's elusive Nancherrow resumes. Time is running out and I am still no closer to solving the mystery.

One of the main questions, now perhaps the only outstanding of my research over these past months, and one which is proving stubbornly difficult to answer, is what or where was the real-life inspiration for Nancherrow, the country house, in *Coming Home*.

The building must be listed, judging by its age and appearance. But there are thousands of buildings in Cornwall on the listed website and they do not by any means all have accompanying photos. Another dead end.

I have tried reverse imaging, using a still from the documentary – zilch.

I decide to phone a friend or rather to ask the experts. Truro Museum are clearly too busy to bother with my bizarre email request sent in with stills of the façade and rambling explanation. Penlee Museum in Penzance are helpful, but nobody can recognize it. The author of *Penzance in 50 Buildings* kindly answers my mail but I have already eliminated his suggestion of Polwithen House.

In desperation, I even put up a poster in my workplace with a £25 reward for any information that might lead to the identification of the house. The only result is that I distract several of my colleagues from their work for a whole afternoon. One even continues after work, ruining a whole evening with relatives on a very kind, but fruitless, search.

Nothing either that I can recognize in Pevsner. In this internet age, the building is certainly keeping a very stealthy profile, so my bet is it is not open to the public.

At the risk of sounding like Kurt Wallander, sometimes I get the vague feeling that I'm missing something, something important that I should have noticed. Something I have seen. But I just can't put my finger on it. It nags at the back of my mind but refuses to pass through to my conscious brain.

There is one final shot and it's a long one. But then all the other trails have gone cold, so it's worth a try.

In *Coming Home*, the house is said to be situated near Rosemullion church. Now there is an area near Helford called Rosemullion, but no church. There is, however, a beautiful church that I visited long ago before my son was born, across the river from Falmouth, St Just in Roselands, which sounds vaguely similar.

It seems a very long way for the young Pilcher to go to play with friends from Penzance or Lelant but the church is special and I would like to include it in this tour of Cornwall, so it's decided.

Patrick Heron impressions

Lighthouse foghorns

12
THE ROSELANDS PENINSULA

(Above) *The Rillaton Cup*

(Right) *Truro Cathedral*

Truro

Our journey to the Roselands Peninsula takes us through Truro.

This small city has a pretty, essentially Georgian, centre and the park with the river running through it, on and past the museum, is well worth a visit. Good shops, too, in the high street for those in need of a touch of retail therapy and a cathedral built in the 1890s by the architect John Pearson that he somehow managed to squeeze into the network of lanes in the centre of the town.

Truro Museum (that is why I am here, leaving Rachel to shop) houses a replica of the Rillaton Cup – the original is in the British Museum, but maybe soon to return, the Curator informs me. This famous gold cup was discovered at Rillaton Barrow near Linkinhorne on Bodmin Moor in 1837.

It is made from corrugated gold sheet and owes its remarkable state of preservation to the fact that it was found inside a pottery vessel. It is thought to date from c1700 BC.

The cup is just inside the first room in a glass case. It's not big, quite small in fact – 3.5 inches high – but it is exquisitely made. It's hard to believe that something of such delicacy and craftsmanship was made almost 4000 years ago.

Those craftsmen were the Celts. Belligerent and barbarian in the classical sense of the word, they were also brilliant artisans and metal-workers.

Rhododendron and church door

Just to fill you in briefly on the backstory. Various populations across Northern and Central Europe are identified as providing strands which all weave together to produce the distinctive Celtic culture. Historians usually start with the Bell-Beaker people (the name derives from their distinctive earthenware) who appear c2600-1900 BC along the banks of the Danube and the Rhine. Then come the Unetice (2300-1600 BC), with their celebrated Nebra Sky disc, thought by some to be a Bronze-Age celestial calculator.

The most recent theory, however, regarding the origins of the Celts turns all the above on its head and posits that initially this people had its roots in the south of Portugal.

Speaking a proto-Celtic language which owed its linguistic foundations to interaction with Phoenician merchants dating back to 900 BC, these Bronze Age traders and sea-farers dealt in silver, copper and tin along the Atlantic coast from the Algarve up past Brittany to Cornwall and beyond to Ireland.

In fact, the latest archaeological evidence, in the shape of characteristic Gundlingen bronze swords found in British excavations, now suggests that, far from Britain submitting to Celtic invasion from modern-day Germany and Switzerland, the Celtic culture spread in fact east from the Atlantic seabord towards Central Europe where this weapon design was adapted to the discovery of the new metal, iron

The Halstatt Celts (this time named after a village in Austria) are the ones who move Europe into the Iron Age[8]. Their need for raw materials draws them westward towards Marseilles, eager to get their hands on the ore passing through the port. At this point, the slightly irked Greeks coin a name for the newcomers: Keltoi – the other-, the hidden-, or the tall-ones, depending on which translation you go with. The Celts have arrived.[15]

Migration towards, and trade with, Cornwall took place throughout this period. The Nebra Sky disc is concrete evidence of that. Recent analysis of its component metals found that the gold of the celestial motifs and the tin used in the making of the bronze were both from the region. Initially, it was thought to be an elaborate hoax, the green patina having been created using urine, hydrochloric acid and a blow torch (a potentially risky process) but now its authenticity is widely accepted by experts.

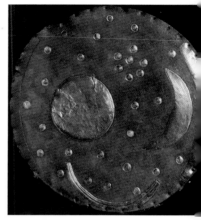

The Nebra Sky Disc.
Photo: Anagoria. Permission – GNU Free Documentation Licence (Wikipedia)

(Left) Stream running through Truro

(Right) Lanes around the cathedral

King Harry's Ferry in a former life

(Below) King Harry's Ferry

There is, in fact, growing evidence that Cornwall was a centre of metal-working and ore production from the earliest times. What makes the Rillaton Cup even more interesting is its similarity stylistically to Aegean metalwork of the period, in particular to finds made at the Greek site of Mycenae.

The cup was passed on as treasure hoard to the crown in the person of William IV and entered the Royal collection. Victoria and Albert had it in their showcases in Osborne on the Isle of Wight. It then seems to go off the radar. It was only after the death of King George V that the cup resurfaced. It was in the King's dressing room. He had been using it to hold his collar studs.

Museum visit over, we make our way through wooded countryside to the King Harry ferry. The River Fal can be glimpsed off to the right through the trees. Past the gardens of Trelissick, the road curves down to the slipway, where the bright blue ferry, looking more like a section of floating bridge, is just coming in. Quite why the ferry is called King Harry is open to discussion – though one story links Henry VIII, the castle which he built at St Mawes just down the road, and Anne Boleyn, in a honeymoon-type situation.

The chain takes up the slack and creaking and clanking we move slowly across.

St Just in Roseland

You enter the churchyard from above – the church stands down below right on the banks of a creek of Carrick Sound. It is this very unusual location that makes the place so special.

You meander along paths, over bridges, crossing streams, all the while in the midst of azaleas, rhododendrons, magnolias, hydrangeas, gunnera, Chinese fan palms, red cedars and more. H. V. Morton, in his *In Search of England*, written in the 1920s wrote, "I have blundered into a Garden of Eden that cannot be described in pen or paint. There is a degree of beauty that flies so high that no net of words or snare of colour can hope to capture." Betjeman concurs. Pevsner is, well, Pevsner. This is not your usual church surrounded by a graveyard; it's a graveyard that is a magical garden with a church somewhere in the middle.

There are dedications to the departed of the most touching kind: two small headstones, side by side, for two twin boys, stick in the memory. A poem by Thomas Brown on a granite slab set in the wall attempts to sum up the feeling of the place (see below). Not the greatest poetry, but it renders the idea.

(Above) Flowers around church door

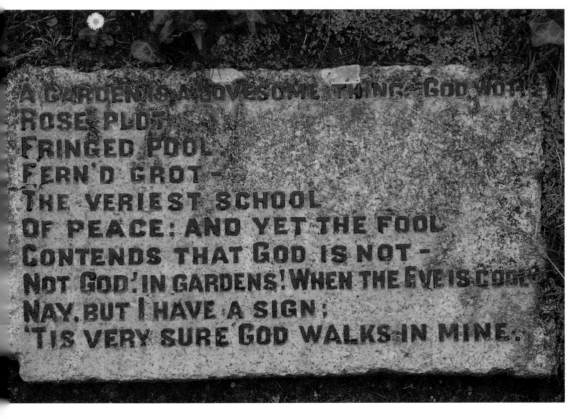

(Left) Garden poem by Thomas Brown

(Far Left) St Just in Roseland church tower

109

Headstones in the churchyard

The label tree

You find yourself bizarrely thinking: if I died, I would like to lie here, on the banks of this river, surrounded by bamboo, palms, tree ferns and camellias. It certainly is one of the most beautiful churchyards I have seen, in the same league as the cemetery above Zurich where James Joyce is buried, but more welcoming, more homely, luxuriant and informal, more peaceful – and the church, although a modest player, does make a difference.

Boards inside tell that the church was founded c550 AD in honour of St Just the Martyr and was served for the next 400 years by Celtic clergy from the cell of Lanzeague. At which point, it was taken by the Saxon Bishops of Cornwall, Crediton and Exeter. There then follows a roll of honour of all the Rectors of the church starting with William de Sancto Justo in 1265, right down to the present incumbent, Kenneth John Boullier. Quite a pedigree.

Outside again, we discover some wonderful slate tombstones with naïve representations of the departed. And, more recent, a tree, hung with labels and simple prayers – "Please keep my family safe and well", reads one.

Grave with rhododendrons

Stained glass window and hat

St Mawes

St Mawes

Although, by now, I have already established that there are no contenders for Nancherrow in the vicinity (Rosteague had a garden which seemed right from the satellite image, but the building was totally wrong) we carry on just to get a look at St Mawes, a popular destination with Prince Charles, as I remember.

We just do a drive-through but I feel it lacks the intimacy of a Dartmouth or a Fowey, too sprawled out, as it is, along the banks of the estuary. We will have to come back and investigate further another time. Anyway, the Prince obviously appreciates it – but then perhaps you would if your thirteenth great-grand-uncle had built the castle.

Trelissick

Looking down to the Fal estuary from Trelissick House.

Another ferry ride and back on the other side again, we realise there is still time to visit somewhere else before returning to St Ives for dinner. Trelissick is National Trust and we have just become members again, so we decide to take advantage.

Trelissick had quite humble farm-house beginnings until it was bought by copper magnate Ralph "Guinea-a-minute" Daniell in 1813. He lavished money on the estate and grounds and when his son, Thomas, took over the reins, he continued in the same vein. It was Thomas who added the rather incongruous portico with ionic columns. The mining slump of the 1830s, coupled with his prodigious extravagance, completely wiped him out. At which point, he had no option but to decamp to France. By 1844, new owner, John Gilbert had the estate on a more even keel and it was he and his son who initiated the planting with flora brought in from Australia.

At the time we visit, the portico is under wraps and being restored. Inside there is an exhibition on Ida Copeland, who took over the estate in 1937 from her step-father. Her husband was director of Spode-Copeland bone china. Her deep interest and involvement in social issues and women's rights meant that she decided to stand for MP for Stoke-on-Trent in the 1931 elections, defeating Oswald Mosely. For this she ought to be remembered if for nothing else.

We take a walk around the gardens which look out over the Fal estuary. It is only later when the holiday is finished that I realise that Trelissick – Tresillick in the book - is the place where Penelope and Richard (it belonged to the mother of a friend of his) in *The Shell Seekers* spend their one-week idyllic break, away from everything. The week ends with Richard revealing that the very next day he must leave on his secret mission; all the training is now over and the moment has arrived.

There is only one small factual problem with the novel's version of events: at the time, the whole of the countryside here was swarming with American troops preparing for D-Day, the area was sealed off to anyone without passes and the 776th Anti-Aircraft Artillery Battalion were actually occupying the house!

Just a quick look round the inevitable Trust shop and Rachel decides to buy, for somewhere in the garden, a very large, bronze-brown metal heron, which eyes us suspiciously from the back seat all the way back to St Ives.

(Below) A floral exhibition   *(Right) Rhododendrons*

(Left) Escallonia and (Right) Rhododendrons

Botanicum

Rosamunde Pilcher clearly loves her gardens and countryside. Many are the plants, flowers and trees of Cornwall that appear in the novels. A list (probably not exhaustive) would include rhododendrons, hawthorn, gorse, thrift (sea pinks), roses (even one called Rosamunde), gunnera, mesembryanthemum, monterey pines, crocus, snowdrops, foxgloves, mallow, honeysuckle, ragged-robin and aconites. There is, however, one that appears in every single novel: escallonia.

Escallonia is a shrub native to the temperate regions of South America. It is found mainly on hill slopes and exposed coasts in the Andes region, which explains why it does so well in Cornwall. It would have made Cousin Jacks working over there feel just that little bit more at home, though Cornish miners saw to it that locals were also introduced to pasties, saffron buns, Methodism and even football, in all the far-flung places that they emigrated to.

Escallonia has a particular property in that, if you crush the leaves between your fingers, a characteristic odour is released. Pilcher invariably describes the scent as "tangy". I think it smells of bergamot; my daughters thought "spicy" or "like tagine". The perfume is also released when the leaves get wet after rain, too.

13

FROM WOOLF TO BETJEMAN

Godrevy Lighthouse

First and foremost, a caveat for Virginia Woolf fans. By all means, drive out to see the lighthouse. But be warned – it will change the memory that you have always had of it. By that, I mean that image of something small, remote and isolated, not of this world, but of a world of fiction, flickering in the distance across the bay. It will become a lighthouse. Not The Lighthouse. As James says in the novel, having waited ten years to get to the island, "So that was the Lighthouse, was it?"

The house, which stands roughly 300 metres off Godrevy Head, was built in 1858. Its construction was prompted by the wreck of the SS *Nile* on the Stones Reef four years before. She was lost with all hands. The light today can be seen from up to 15 kilometres and flashes white/red every ten seconds, though if you are seeing it red, you have got problems, as the red is only visible if you have strayed into the arc of danger from the reef.

Woolf (what would the world do without Wikipedia?) first visited in September 1892 – she would have been ten and a half. She signed the visitors' book and in so doing enabled a Bonham's auctioneer to bring down the hammer in 2011 and sell said book for £10,250.

I am not sure why Woolf decided to move the whole situation to the Hebrides, but I did discover that her mother, who was involved in all sorts of philanthropic activities, did, in fact, organise the delivery of used magazines to the Godrevy light, just as happens in the novel.

As has happened in other places, what struck me most while we were there was not directly connected to the main object of the visit.

There is a bench (my granny would have called it "a form") looking out over the ocean which is beautifully lettered and carved, with the inscription KEN BRAY ICE CREAM VAN MAN 1989-2009.

Godrevy Lighthouse

The ice cream van man

An atmospheric vintage postcard of the Godrevy Light

I have summer flash-backs of 99's, Sky Rays, Zooms, Splits and Mivvis (Pineapple Mivvis!), Tip-Tops and Jubblies sucked until just colourless ice; the forever financially-out-of-reach Heart.

Perhaps the cruellest story I have ever heard is the one where parents tell their child that when you hear the chime of a van going past, it means that the ice cream man has in fact run out of ice-cream for the day.

Returning in February 2019, my Woolf "moment" over, on a magnificent bright, clear day, I would now wholeheartedly advise you to go out to the point, not least for the wonderful sight, at Mutton Bay, of the colony of grey seals. A real high-point.

Godrevy grey seal colony, Mutton Bay

At Godrevy Point

116

(Left) Hell's Mouth

Hell's Mouth

Hell's Mouth is a deep inlet in the cliffs, just north of Godrevy, where waves are funnelled in and break spectacularly on the rocks below.

The mouth is formed in the shape of a devil's cauldron and, like any self-respecting cauldron, the rim at the top is narrower compared to the pot itself. This presents a problem. It means that, to get a good photo of what's going on down below at crashing wave level, a certain amount of peering over the cliff edge is involved.

My photos will not show this sea level action, I'm afraid. I don't know if it is the same for all sufferers of vertigo, but I find that the closer I get to the edge, the more I feel drawn towards it. I have even had to sit down on occasions to prevent myself going over.

A woman just a few metres along the cliff has a novel way of getting a better shot. She leans out towards the chasm, I-phone in hand, while her girlfriend counterbalances her by pulling her back with her handbag. Today, fortunately, that's not an option for me: 1. I'm on my own and 2: I don't have my handbag with me anyway.

(Right) Close to the edge!

117

Sadly, it seems that Hell's Mouth is also a renowned suicide location. The senior coroner for Cornwall, Dr Emma Carlyon, made recommendations in a report in 2016 in order to prevent future deaths. She appeals to support groups such as Samaritans to provide telephone numbers at the spot, as there are at Beachy Head, and also asks the National Trust to use natural barriers such as gorse to possibly dissuade people.

Back at home, I come across a harrowing piece of You Tube footage – a landslide in 2011 that happened only metres from where I had been standing. Take a look: https://www.youtube.com/watch?v=QdsxtCtX5nk

Absolutely amazing, and terrifying. Be careful.

Bedruthan Steps, wow #3

Bedruthan Steps

Our next stop is Bedruthan Steps. The Victorians would travel in their carriages to stand at the top of the original rock-hewn zig-zag staircase cut into the cliff face. This has long since disappeared, but the name has remained.

The various iconic "stacks" along the beach all have their own names, too. Fourth along from where I am standing, for example, is Samaritan Island, so named because during a storm on 21 October 1846, the 220-ton brig *Samaritan* was wrecked here. The ship was bound for Constantinople with a cargo of brightly-patterned silk and cotton cloth. Once the locals got wind of the event, a three-day frenzy of "wrecking" ensued – one account tells of 1000 villagers involved, including "men who stand up in the pulpit". Neighbourhood churches would have probably boasted some of the finest-attired and gaily-dressed congregations in the country in the years that followed.

Later I discover that I haven't taken my photos from the place where the most celebrated views are to be had (the top of the staircase) but from Carnewas Island – a classic case of rushing in without checking.

My oversight has a justification. The reason being that I got carried away with the moment – this was, in fact, wow #3.

Padstow

We continue on to Padstow, on the banks of the Camel estuary.[16]

As we wind our way down the hill, the enormous pile of the Metropole dominates the entry into the town. It's another example of a hotel built by the railways, this time the London and South Western, in order to accommodate the arrival of new visitors to the area in 1899.

Part of the station still survives in the first of the several car parks that we try to find a space in; a car park flanked by the timber-clad building of Rick Stein's Cookery School. This sentence, as it happens, rather neatly sums up the town – it's very difficult to find a space to park, and almost equally as difficult to get away from Mr Stein.

I came many years ago to eat at Rick Stein's sea-food restaurant and had imagined that, in the interim, the town would have gone right up-market, but there are a surprising number of families around, and there's a real bucket-and-spade atmosphere, which I love. I get the feeling that Rock, the town that stands on the other side of the estuary, has

(Below) Padstow harbour

Looking over to Rock from Padstow

The ice cream van man

become the new in-place to go for the boating set, and you can always pop back across if you want to savour Rick's fayre.

The celebrity chef has been accused of trying to take over the town. His empire includes The Seafood Restaurant, St Petroc's Bistro, Rick Stein's Café and Stein's Fish and Chips. Then he has three Stein-themed shops; a deli, a patisserie and a gift shop. He also owns the Padstow Seafood Cookery School and four hotels. Oh, and he brews the local beer – Chalky's Bite – named after his beloved ex-Russell Terrier who used to accompany him on all his TV travels.

His supporters will point out that his businesses employ over 450 people in the town. From a personal point of view, I have to admit that I quite like the chap. His Sardinian slow roasted belly of pork with fennel seeds, garlic and rosemary is the most-loved recipe I have ever cooked. I think his slightly awkward talk to camera in his travel documentaries is great – and his interview with the Dalai Lama is brilliant.

Again, on the down side, and this is a serious one, the Stein-effect has attracted more wealthy second-home owners to the town and pushed up property prices, making it almost impossible now for young locals to get a foot on the property ladder – a phenomenon that is happening all over Cornwall.

These youngsters would not, however, be the first locals to leave the area in search of a better life elsewhere. 250,000 Cornish left the country between 1861 and 1901. A veritable diaspora. When it came to emigration, Padstow as a port came third only after Liverpool and London. Driven by lack of work and the appalling working conditions and rock-bottom wages in the mines, they left in their droves for South Africa, South America, and Australia. Free passage was often offered, as, for example, to Canada. It got to the point where the joke was that a mine is a hole anywhere in the world with at least one Cornishman at the bottom.

There was even a fair proportion of Cornish miners amongst the 49ers in the Californian gold rush.

And, almost inevitably, records show that there were also tinners, hoping to make good in the USA, on the missing persons list of the *Titanic*.

Finally, for our German-speaking readers, a note about "the one that got away" on our visit to Padstow.

Prideaux Place, on the outskirts of the town, is an Elizabethan stately home dating back to 1592. It has been the uninterrupted home to the Prideaux family for 14 generations. Far too grand to feature in any of Pilcher's oeuvre, it has, nonetheless (coinciding as it does with our Teutonic friends' imagined perception of what an English country house should be like), been the backdrop to at least 14 German Rosamunde Pilcher film specials.

So, whereas after Sunday dinner, we might be sitting down to *Vera* grappling with county lines and cuckoo's nests, in Switzerland and Germany they would be tuning in to *Engaged and Confused* (2011), *Promises and Lies* (2104) or *A Doctor and Three Women* (2017) – a selection of titles filmed at Prideaux which give a hint of the slightly racy territory the German TV company are taking viewers into with their R.P. franchise.

And, it transpires, Peter Prideaux-Brune, the current double-barrelled Lord of the Manor, has a Hitchcockesque penchant for cameo roles in the productions, having so far played a chauffeur, a coroner and a gin-taster.

I have mentioned elsewhere that we are on a tight schedule in Cornwall and, despite various phone and email exchanges with Peter's friendly P.A., our would-be thespian is proving tricky to tie down for a brief interview. What's more, the day we are due in Padstow, the house is, exceptionally, closed to the public for a children's charity event. It's a pity, but something to pencil in for the second edition.

Crabbing with Dad

Buckets and spades

Fish and chips

121

Up-market fish fayre

St Enodoc (and Rock and Trebetherick)

Rock, across the water, is the domain of Nathan Outlaw, a 2-star Michelin chef, who as a twenty-year-old was an apprentice to Rick Stein. He now has his own restaurant at St Enodoc's Hotel and also has the glass-balconied Mariners Public House, right opposite Padstow, above the ferry slipway. We have a brief drink at the latter, looking out over the estuary at the various comings and goings on the landing-craft-cum-ferryboat, before making the short journey on to Trebetherick and St Enodoc's church.

Waiting at a junction on the way out of town, it's like watching a catwalk of luxury SUVs. BMWs, Jaguars, Lexus, Audi Q7s and Porsche Cayenne process past. A quick glance at Rightmove.co.uk tells you what's up for sale today on the property market: apart from building plots from half a million upwards, there's a 3-bedroom flat (with panoramic sea views) at £695,000 and a 4-bedroom detached house (views of estuary and golf course) at £1,650,000.

Trebetherick (and happy summers spent there) was immortalised in Betjeman's eponymous poem, that of "sand in the sandwiches, wasps in the tea". Treen, in Daymer Lane, next to the golf course was Betjeman's holiday home that he bought in 1959. Locals claim that wild parties regularly took place here. It was here, in fact, that Betjeman died in 1984. Torquil, as the house is called today, is now a holiday let. It sleeps 11 in six bedrooms. It is described as having space for late-night revelry as well as a space for quiet contemplation upstairs. Price is £1285 per week in the low season, rising to £4400 in high – not bad for 11 people, I suppose – a bit steep if there's just the two of you.

St Enodoc's church has a couple of typically Cornish characteristics: 1) It's in the middle of a golf course, and 2) It has suffered considerably in the past from wind-blown dunes. In fact, for almost 300 years it was all but buried. To maintain the tithes required by the church, it had to hold a service at least once a year when vicar and congregation would be lowered into position through a hole in the roof. The situation was finally resolved in 1864 and the church emerged sphinx-like from the sands of time.

We park at the start of the path signposted "Church".

Someone is practising their tenor sax off to our left. The large house to the right has an enormous garden whose immaculate lawn stretches across to a stream that in a leisurely way meanders along the edge of the property. There is a gazebo set up where guests will collect their drinks and canapés before they spill out on to the grass for that last party of the summer. A child's swing is suspended from the bough of an enormous centuries-old cedar centre left.

I can hear Rachel's mind whirring as she contemplates the scene. I wonder to myself about how a life can pass so quickly – why did I never set my sights on a house like this? Inability? Too much the dreamer? The waster? Too shy, too timid? Other values and things to do? I settle, as usual, on the last explanation.

On the way to St Enodoc church

The crumpled spire

Back to reality – as the path begins to cross the golf-course there is a sign warning of incoming balls from the right. Basically, you're looking out for poor first drives off the 12th, and then, nearer the church, for over-cooked approach shots from players on the 10th. Betjeman, himself, was an enthusiastic, if not proficient, member of the club and, of course, wrote a poem, *Seaside Golf*, about his experiences playing the 13th hole.

Now, If there's one thing I have learnt from Niklaus (Pevsner) it's that a steeple on a church is a very rare sight in Cornwall. And the one protruding from the vegetation in the distance is crooked – like the cow with a crumpled horn.

It's a fair way to the church (sorry). I imagine a wedding party. Women with their dresses blowing in the wind holding on to their hats – like in a Jane Austen novel or is it Thackeray? – strung out along the path between the 8th and 9th. Occasionally ducking at the shout of "Fore!" The expectant vicar at the lych gate hearing the sound of laughter and voices carried on the wind.

And what about funerals – do they rotate teams of pall-bearers?

We spoke about Sir John's grave over breakfast with Clair at the Tinners Arms. He is just on the right as you go in, opposite her in-laws. Clair, it turns out, does the flowers at the church (helped by Florence).

In my (usual) enthusiasm, I forget to get the classic shot of the church nestled in the golf course looking seawards from the hillock behind. There is his grave, though – the lettering on the headstone just a tad florid for my taste.

The entrance to the churchyard is through the lych-gate I mentioned, lych being the old Saxon word for corpse. In the middle ages, before the time of refrigeration, the dead, when they died at home, were taken on a bier to the gate, where they remained, even one or two days, watched over by the vigil-keepers until the funeral could take place. In some churches, as here, there is large flat stone, a lych-stone, upon which the body, usually just wrapped in a shroud, was laid.

Betjeman's funeral has stuck in local memory because of the appalling weather that day. His coffin was carried, underslung, in torrential rain all along the 10th hole followed by a large, very wet crowd of London literary journalists.

The lych gate

John Betjeman's headstone

Inside the church, what I remember most (apart from the wonderful flowers), is a slate tablet on the south wall commemorating a shipwreck. As everything else inside the church is of considerable antiquity, it is a shock when you read that these three crew members perished on 30 May 1995 on the coast just two and a half miles from here. At the time, the *Maria Asumpta* was the oldest surviving sailing ship in the world, having been launched in 1858. Judged to be guilty of negligence for sailing (against expert advice) too close to a lee shore, the captain was jailed for eighteen months. This poignant relief-carving is by Phillip Chatfield, one of the survivors.

(Below) The Maria Asumpta

IN MEMORY OF
EMILY MACFARLANE   JOHN SHANNON   ANNE TAYLOR
WHO PERISHED ON 30TH MAY 1995 WHEN THE BRIG
MARIA ASUMPTA WAS WRECKED ON THE RUMPS
TWO AND A HALF MILES NORTH OF THIS CHURCH

14

TALES OF ORE AND WONDER

St Michael's Mount and Marazion

This time when we come down the road into Penzance we take a left towards Marazion. The last night of this stay in Cornwall is going to be at the Mount Haven. I have booked a room with a view over St Michael's Mount, explaining over the phone to the receptionist that I hope to get some good photos for the book.

We have been given the room right on the far-corner of the building with the best possible view. From the 4-poster bed, you look straight out to the Mount. The island rising out of the sea in front of us is easily the most iconic image to be had in Cornwall. The romantic silhouette we see from this angle was largely the work of one man – architect Piers St Aubyn, in the late 1800s. Even Pevsner effuses, "Spectacular and picturesque", "a sight from some positions reminiscent of Mount Athos or Tibetan monasteries". Curiously, Von Ribbentrop, the Third Reich's Foreign Minister was a fan, too. In the case of a successful invasion of England, he had already pencilled himself in for the Duchy of Cornwall, with, naturally, the Mount as his seat.

On the desk, there is a card with a painting of our view – "Welcome to the Mount Haven" – signed James and Mary St Levan. A nice touch – they must be the owners.

I pop down to reception to say thank you for the room. We get to talking about Rosamunde Pilcher. The previous hotel where the receptionist had worked was often used by German film crews shooting episodes.

(Right) Room with a View

Marazion flowers

Out of the Blue

She had a German colleague there who was absolutely fangirling (new word for me) the actors. Apparently the best-looking in the country are chosen – another reason why Pilcher films are so popular!

As it's still only about four o'clock and we're only here for the one night, we decide to take a walk down into Marazion. If anyone has ever grown up in the shadow of a high-performing older (or younger) sibling they will understand how Marazion feels. It's a nice row of houses basically; cute shops, a pub; a little rough round the edges, with a tremendous, gob-smacking view.

The black volcanic bed rock that has risen up to form the Mount is exposed on the sands. It's a geological miniature of what happened throughout Cornwall. The magma dome pushed up through the overlying sedimentary rocks, producing Bodmin and Penwith Moors, and here on a smaller scale the Mount. And there are mini tin lodes here, too, produced by the contact of the molten rock with its surroundings. As we reach the beach, the tide is coming in and the last section of the causeway out to the Mount is just about to disappear. The sky has turned an ominous leaden grey. Three young boys are making a desperate last-ditch attempt to stop the waves from breaching the sand walls of their castle. An Italian woman is paddling out along the causeway into the sea, talking all the while to her friend back on land – a sort of walking-on-water stunt for Facebook or Instagram, I presume.

(Left) The Mount from the hotel   *The Mount rises up*

The sun is out again

Twenty minutes later, and, as is often the case in this part of the world, as evening draws on, the sun has flooded out under the clouds illuminating the warm biscuit-brown of the castle granite. And now it's a young auburn-haired girl who is running into the sea fully-clothed. It must be something in the water down here.

That evening we dine in the hotel restaurant and I have the best dish of the trip so far: a starter of crispy breaded mackerel, remoulade puree, watercress and beets – exquisite.

Before turning in, I read up about the legendary island of Ictis. It is first mentioned by Herodotus in 445 BC who refers to the British Isles as the Cassiterides or the Tin Islands. Publius Crassus, a Roman Official – Rome was getting interested by then – describes it thus,

"The inhabitants of that part of Britain, which is called Belerion, are very fond of strangers and from their intercourse with foreign merchants are civilised in their manner of life. They prepare the tin, working very carefully the earth in which it is produced. The ground is rocky but it contains earthy veins, the produce of which is ground down, smelted and purified. They beat the metal into masses shaped like knuckle-bones and carry it off to a certain island off Britain called Iktis. During the ebb of the tide the intervening space is left dry and they carry over to the island the tin in abundance in their wagons… Here, merchants buy the tin from the natives and carry it over to Gaul, and after travelling overland for about thirty days, they finally bring their loads on horses to the mouth of the Rhone."

As to its location, there are several contenders for the title. Looe with its offshore island is a possibility (they also claim a visit by Joseph of Arimathea accompanied by Jesus[17]). Devon points to Mount Batten Island off Plymouth and Burgh Island of Agatha Christie fame (here ancient tin ingots were actually discovered on the sea bed at the mouth of the River Erme). Then there's also the Isle of Wight. And, of course, there's St Michael's Mount.

The Mount at night

Looking out of the window now, at the island lit up in the moonlight, I feel certain it was here. I would like to think that Phoenician ships used to arrive off the coast laden with richly-coloured cloth, earthenware, glass, wine, saffron and bracelets. And when they left, their holds would be piled high with their precious metal cargo. I see them returning to their homelands, landing in Cadiz, Malaga, or Palermo – the mariners regaling their wide-eyed listeners with tales of giant blue chieftains,[18] the custodians of the sacred ore, living on an island permanently swathed in mists, at the ends of the earth.

Early morning traffic in the English Channel

I wake early and lie listening to the sounds of the morning as the sun comes up. A massed choir of songbirds has gathered to perform outside. There is twittering, tweeting and trilling; chirping and whistling. A crow caws irritatedly, annoyed by the show-offs. In the background, I can hear the sound of the waves on the shore below. But it's the birds that demand your attention – calling and answering, some insistently repetitive, some a lilting refrain, gurgling and fluid; pipit, pipit, pipit, a quick-fire burst of screeched trills, followed by a single punctuating chirp – a dying coda.

Down in Marazion, we ask for information from a vicar chatting in the car park. Our chaplain (as it turns out) is off to do the 11.15 service up at the castle. He tells us it's a fantastic place, but quite a trek up there. As the tide is in, he directs us to a small launch which does the run to the island.

We alight exactly where Queen Victoria did in 1846, her petite shoe-print immortalized on the quay. Her Majesty and His Royal Highness walked up to the castle and Albert played the organ in the chapel for her.

(Above) In Victoria's footsteps

(Left) A mackerel sky – the weather's changing

The village on the Mount

The small row of cottages is home to the 35 or so people who make up what must be one of the country's smallest parishes. The population used to be more numerous. Sir John St Aubyn, the third baronet, who made a fortune from mining, built 53 houses here in the 1800s for all the people associated with the industry. Roughly 300 in all. There were three schools and, seems about right, three pubs.

We buy our tickets and purchase a guidebook. OK, I see – so James St Aubyn, the Lord of the Manor, is the self-same Baron St Levan – the one who owns the hotel.

Construction of the priory atop the mount first started in 1135, under the watchful eye of Bernard le Bec, the Abbot of Mont St Michel in Normandy. At this stage of its history, the island was under French control. One theory is that this stint away from home was a way of testing the young novices to see if, faced with the rigueurs and hardships of Cornwall, their vows of devotion to the French mother order would waver.

(Left) The Blue Room

(Middle) Stained glass window

(Right) We are a long way up! – looking back towards Marazion

St Michael doing what he does best

In 1414, after warring with France for 100 years, Henry V decided that this was a connection best severed and the priory came back under English control.

The reason for all this religious interest in the first place was down to the fact that St Michael, no less, was said to have been seen by fishermen on the Penzance side of the Mount in 495 AD. A brief aside – St Michael, as one American website puts it, is "God's top angel", so technically he's not really a saint. Anyway, be he saint or angel, his two main duties are: 1) to combat Satan and 2) to call men at life's end to their heavenly judgment, and then escort the lucky ones to heaven. As all this takes place on high, it is churches and chapels on the summits of hills, mountains and the like, that usually come in for his attention. He also finds time to be patron saint of soldiers, the police and doctors.

Once arrived on the top (it is quite a climb) it's the Blue Drawing Room and the various examples of stained glass that stick in my memory. And I liked the small bronze statue of St Michael in the chapel, by Lyn Constable Maxwell. His sword is raised and he is treading underfoot (as usual) Lucifer but (unusually) he is offering him a hand of mercy at the same time. I am not sure if the real Saint Michael would have approved.

Out on the terrace designed by Piers St Aubyn, the views down to the gardens below are vertiginous. Although I fancy myself as a bit of a horticulturalist, the particular skill-set needed to work as a gardener here would preclude my ever applying for a post. Abseiling, it seems, is a key requirement when a significant proportion of your weeds – brambles and the like – are growing out of sheer rock faces, tens of metres above the ground. The guidebook informs us, however, that the gardeners here love it.

I steel myself for another brief look down. Yes, that's definitely a no.

15

THE GIRL ON THE EDGE OF THE CLIFF

Celtic cross

St Buryan

We are just into October and the final day of the last weekend we have available. I have come here to St Buryan to see the Celtic cross in the churchyard. Betjeman devotes a whole B & W photo page to it. Celtic crosses are everywhere in Cornwall but what I have learned is that they are of much more recent date than I previously thought.

Again some background will be useful. The expansion of the Roman Empire had pushed the Celts back to the western fringes – Scotland, Ireland, Wales and Cornwall. From a religious point of view, the Celts were polytheistic, having deities ad libitum with spheres of action ranging from manual skills such as carpentry and metalworking, to natural phenomena such as lightning or topographical features such as rivers.

In 1313 AD, Emperor Constantine issues the edict of Milan which quickly leads to Christianity becoming the official religion of the Roman world. In the fifth century, missionaries from Britain, including the Romano-British St Patrick, carry the word across the Irish Sea, where it blossoms, and soon there are Irish saints sailing across to Cornwall to spread the gospel. Saints whose preaching prowess, it seems, was matched only by their prodigious sea-faring skills – St Ia navigated across the water to St Ives on a leaf, while St Piran, the county's patron saint, made landfall at Perranporth after a long voyage on a mill-stone. The Celts isolated in Cornwall came late to Christianity.

The result of this influx was that worship of natural springs gradually gave way to reverence of Holy Wells and the first monasteries – their locations today often indicated today by the prefix "Lan" in their place-names – were built. With a preference for higher ground, these would become the raised church sites like the one we can see today at St Buryan. The earliest Celtic crosses don't make their appearance till the ninth and tenth centuries and many are of much later date. There are other more ancient standing stones, but they are not crosses.[19]

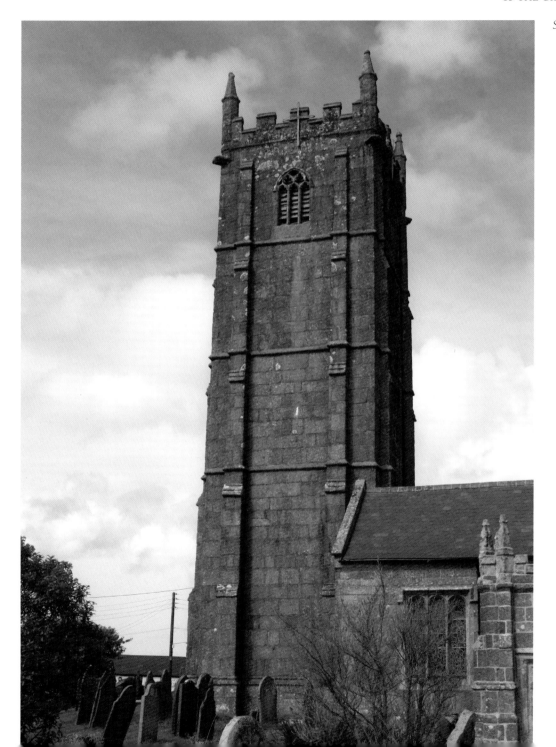

St Buryan church tower

This calf has just been born

(Left) Late-flowering hydrangeas

(Right) Gnarled tree trunk at St Loy

St Loy

We drive a little way along the coast and then head down to the sea. We are going to make one more search for the location of Laura Knight's painting *At the Edge of the Cliff* but this time we are going to come at it along the coast path from the west, hopefully avoiding the need for crampons and carabiners presented by the Lamorna approach.

The path starts to twist down towards St Loy's Cove, supposedly the warmest cove in the whole of the United Kingdom, the mean annual temperature being higher even than the Isles of Scilly.

We are soon seeing the evidence: hydrangeas still in flower, tree ferns, palms and giant leaves of gunnera line the banks of the small stream that we are now following as it cascades down over waterfalls towards the shore. Up through the undergrowth, a wooden bridge crossing the stream is just visible – like something you'd see on a willow-pattern plate.

(Left) Approaching the point

(Right) Heavy-duty flotsam

The stream takes a final tumble over a lintel-like granite block and we are out on the beach. It's not what I expected – no sand, but as far as the eye can see giant, smooth, rounded granite boulders. And also not what I had expected, to our left, and not far away, is the rock formation of the painting. The fractured granite cliff slopes down to the sea only to rise again in a most unusual, almost equilaterally triangular, pinnacle, like a dragon resting its head in the water.

I pull the folded picture out of my pocket. We need to get up there on the dragon's back, then down onto its neck, to look out over the pyramid of rocks extending out into the sea.

Cautiously stepping and hopping from boulder to boulder, we make our way along the beach. Half way along, a huge tripod-shaped hunk of bright orange rusted iron lies up against the base of the cliff. In October 1912, a French steamer, the *Abertay*, ran aground here in thick fog. The crew were amazed to find they were jammed up next to another vessel towering above them on the rocks. Receiving no replies to their shouts, they realized it was abandoned. The SS *America* had itself run aground seven months earlier in the very same spot. The thankful crew were able to clamber off their now-foundering ship, spend the night on the wreck and escape to safety the following morning.

Shortly after, the path leaves the beach and starts to curve its way upwards, along the somewhat muddy bed of a small stream. As the terrain flattens out, we find ourselves in another unusual setting – the path leads through a glade of stunted oak-trees (I have never seen oaks so close to the sea as these before). It's autumn and the leaves are piling up underfoot, but, come spring, I am assured by reliable sources that this section of the path will be awash with blue-bells in a display whose equal – anywhere – you will be hard-pressed to find.

Another steep section and we come out atop our cliff. It's getting warmer – off comes the sweater and the jacket.

The stunted oak wood

139

(Above) These are the rocks in the painting!

This is the place alright. All we need to do now is to get into position and wait for the sun to re-appear. The bright morning has now turned overcast but the clouds are scudding across the sky pretty briskly and soon the small patch of blue over to our right, at first hardly big enough to make a cat a pair of trousers, is opening out and extending as the cover breaks up.

The next forty-five minutes are taken up in as intense a period of scrutiny of sky and clouds as I have ever experienced. On the horizon, a mammoth container ship is bathed in sunlight throughout the wait. Nearer to where we stand, shining pools of light move tantalizingly towards us only to then disappear. Behind us, at one point, the Tater Du lighthouse is brightly illuminated while we remain frustratingly in shade.

Then, slowly, it edges towards us. Now the beginning of our way today is lit up. How marvellous it must be to live in that cottage just back from the beach! Ever closer it comes, and there it is. The rocks take on a wonderful biscuit hue, the sea a deep, deep blue with narrow ribbons of white edging the rocks.

Rachel on the edge of the cliff

Nancherrow III

Just like the painting.

Suddenly it dawns on me. How can I have missed it? It has been there staring at me all the time. How many times have I carried it around folded up in my pocket? How many times have I shown it to people?

The painting. The painting was the key.

What was it Gus says towards the end of the novel? That when it was time for them to go and Loveday turned to watch the sea, he had recognised her as the girl in the Laura Knight painting *At the Edge of the Cliff*, one of his most treasured possessions.

Whether or not Loveday is Gus' girl on the cliff or not is a matter for the characters in the book, but more importantly, what Pilcher is telling the reader with this passage is that this cliff, these rocks are the ones in the painting – *this* is the cove below Nancherrow. As so often in the books – Penjizal is another example – our author has misled us as to the exact location, but the description of how to get there and what the place is like are precise. I realise later that she's even named a character in the book after this rocky promontory.

If I'd had more of a head for heights back at Lamorna, I could have worked this out months ago.

No matter, I now know just where to look. I don't know its real name yet, but I'm 100% certain that when I see a photo, it will be the house in the film.

Time to set off back. I turn to take one last look at the rocks.

Just for a moment, in the distance, across the silvered water, I see Marconi's *Elettra* glide past, sailing westwards.[20]

The Elettra?

Postscript

I remarked to Rachel at the end of our week in Cornwall that we hadn't heard a single Police siren the whole time we were there. And we had seen children walking, swimming, surfing, jumping in the harbour – not one child with an Xbox.

And everyone was so friendly – so here's thanks to: Linda Weir – the Lady in the Van; Andrea and the staff in The Sloop; the staff and owners at Brocante; the ladies at the Tourist Information office in St Ives; the staff in Boots, St Ives; the ladies at the Primitive Methodist Church; Marie of The Firs; the woman at Talland House; the girl with red hair in The Penwith Gallery; the gentleman at The Porthmeor Studios; the waiters and waitresses at the Porthmeor Café; the guy on the desk at The Barbara Hepworth House; Sophie Bowness; the landlord and staff at the Tinner's Arms; the dotty woman at Cape Cornwall; the woman at Land's End reception; the old guy in the tourist information centre at Penzance; the lady in Penzance who saw my camera and told me to look out for the Egyptian House in Chapel Street; the man at the café at Lamorna cove; the lady at The Apple Tree Café; the guy at the Lizard – who gave us a free booklet "cos you're such nice people"; the curator of the Truro museum and Mandy; the receptionist and all the staff at Mt Haven; the Chaplain (off to do the 11.15 service in the chapel on the Mount) and the man in the car park at Marazion; the staff at St Michael's Mount shop and ticket office; Sue and John, for their marvellous hospitality; Julia our resident stable-door expert; Poppy at Richard Green Galleries for her help; April Brooks and Jason Calder, St Ives Society of Artists; Beth Woolway and Arwen Fitch, Tate St Ives; Alessandra Serri (Tate Britain); Jasmin at DACS; Jan Bright and Sophie Fraser (she's the one with the red hair) at Penwith Galleries.

End Notes

[1] Apart from names for rivers and place-names, only a handful of Celtic words have made it through to modern English: ass, basket, beak, brock, coomb, crag, dad, dun, flannel, gob, nook, tor and even, apparently, whisky.

[2] A voiceless velar fricative, my learned colleague informs me

[3] An interesting linguistic point: France, Spain, Italy and Portugal whose concrete, practical ties with the region go far back have a translation in their own language for the county, respectively, Les Cornouailles, Cornualles, La Cornovaglia and Cornualha. The Germans who came late to the party through Wagner's very spiritual, sublimated version of the Cornish Tristan and Isolde draught and more recently with their own take on Rosamunde Pilcher's Cornwall have no word of their own for the county.

[4] Beling wrote three books in German to accompany his TV series back at the end of the 1990s – the first *Enchanting Cornwall* deals with the locations of, and anecdotes associated with, the first batch of TV films. The second *Cornwall – Garden Paradise* looks at the gardens and the stately homes that often go with them – your Mt Edgecumbes and Lanhydrocks, your Trellisicks and Trebahs; the last, and here perhaps we are getting to the heart (or stomach?) of the matter: *Leben und Geniessen in Cornwall* (Live and Enjoy Cornwall) which basically lists the best things you can eat and where you can eat them in the county and is accompanied by numerous recipes of delicious local specialities.

Mark Pilcher, the author's youngest son, puts the success down to the quality of the filming. This invariably has long drone-sequences of sun-flooded clifftops with the hero in sun-glasses at the wheel of his Morgan while he talks to his heroine whose long brown hair is blowing in the sea-breeze

Robin Pilcher, the author's eldest son, writing in an article in the magazine *My Cornwall* comes up with an interesting idea which ties in with things I have noticed in the films. His opinion is, after making it clear that his mother's novels are not romantic novels but remarkable studies into family life and relationships, that German tourists have a sense of nostalgia for when Germany and England had very close ties, values and culture because they shared the same royal family i.e. Victoria and company and the Hanoverians. His mother's films have helped to heal the rift caused by the two World Wars.

The Weimar Republic in 1919 put an end to the German nobility, whereas in Britain it is still possible to visit and meet landowners still living in their piles, a world which your normal German has never had access to. This explains why Peter Prideaux-Brune's house at Prideaux Place outside Padstow is such a massive draw for German film crews and German tourists alike. And also why the film directors always have to aggrandize Pilcher's rather humble country houses. When an English company made the film *Coming Home* starring Peter O'Toole and Joanna Lumley in 1999, the top roles went to

English actors but, as it was a joint production with Germany, German actors got some minor parts and the Germans were also allowed to upgrade Nancherrow from a Cornish country house (which I am still trying to identify somewhere on the Cornish peninsula) to the mega Wrotham Park in Hertfordshire.

The Germans have got their own back recently providing minor roles for English actors and extras in their TV films. Dennis, a friend of a friend in Torquay, was stopped one day at the lights while driving his racing-green Landrover which the film scout wanted to requisition as a gardener's vehicle. He had to keep the fictitious company's signs on – "Cavendish and Son Est.1955" – for four weeks. The Landrover apparently was used in the film for a liaison with a gardener and the lady of the manor, which sounds more like D.H. Lawrence than Rosamunde Pilcher. The TV company seem to have a franchise, now producing their own material. The film crew also had their eye on Dennis' dog, a border collie, who is now on stand-by for an episode next year.

[5] The colour, in fact, comes from an orange coloured anthraquinone pigment called parietin that forms tiny crystals in the top layer of the lichen. The synthesis of parietin is enhanced by UV-B, that is, short wave ultraviolet B. Basically, sunlight. In layman's terms, the more sun this stuff gets the more orange it becomes. And that's just what you feel when you look down on St Ives – this is a sunny place – and it's the lichen that's telling you.

[6] Although he was subsequently discovered to be in the Nazi "black book", a list of some 2800 anti-German propagandists who were to be immediately detained by the SS in the case of a German invasion of England (Virginia Woolf was also on the list as was Sigmund Freud although he already died the year before) as Pevsner's official papers hadn't come through he became classified as an Alien – category C – low risk.

It was scant appreciation for someone who would go on to produce one of the most famous of English guidebooks. But – as D.H. Lawrence was to find out too – this was the climate in the country in 1940 after Dunkirk. Shortly after the evacuation, a Minister speaking on The BBC announced "Be careful at this moment how you put complete trust in any person of German or Austrian connections. If you know people of this kind who are still at large, keep your eye on them; they may be perfectly all right – but they may not."

The German invasion of Paris and the Battle of Britain ratchetted the tension up even more, and at the end of June 1940, Pevsner found himself no. 54829 at an Alien Internee Camp near Liverpool. In these camps there were a disproportionate number of academics and professionals and conditions were not ideal. At one location, it was reported that there were no more than 60 buckets provided for the bodily functions of

2000 people. As one commentator noted, you could see men of European reputation in an act which is normally not performed in public.

[7] There are various other possible reasons for starting with Cornwall:

1. After the rigours of the war, Pevsner was anxious to get totally away from the bomb-scarred capital to a bit of bucolic peace and quiet with partner Lola.

2. Petrol was still in short supply after wartime and Cornwall simply didn't have that much, from an architectural point of view to see, so not much driving – a fact which Pevsner is quick to point out in the very first sentence of this first slim volume

3. (A.N. Wilson's version) – Teutonic thoroughness – he wanted to start in the bottom left hand corner and work his way systematically around the country.

[8] Pre-nineteenth century, they were immersed for their protection in a solution made from the bark of oak trees, hence the term barking. After 1840 this was replaced by cutch, a product from the trunks of Indian acacia trees which produced a tar-like substance which was used to coat the nets.

[9] I have recently come across another interesting theory, with anecdotal evidence to back it up: the pilchards were frightened away by noise, the noise of the railway. The two dates: arrival of trains and disappearance of fish do tally closely.

[10] Interestingly, for other reasons, I have been doing some research into Garum recently, the fish sauce/oil so loved by the Romans and so popular throughout the ancient world. This was actually made from the innards of anchovies, sardines etc and again was notoriously smelly, (it is odd how so many foods prized for their taste combine it with the most horrible stink – think durian or surstromming). They still make a version of Garum in present day Italy – Colatura di Alici. So again in the interests of research, I purchased a bottle from Amazon. The briefest of sniffs (that is a warning) of the liquid will give you an extremely close idea of how St Ives smelt 200 years ago.

[11] It was on this visit, too, that I discovered that a long, low, white sofa that I had coveted from first sight when I visited Kettles Yard as an undergraduate at the end of the '70s, and that during the 18 or so following years while living in Italy I had searched for in all manner of furniture shops, coming close to buying on more than one occasion expensive but never quite right simulacrums, was in fact simply two small single beds joined together by Jim Ede.

[12] **A bluffer's guide to tin mining**

Adit – a shaft or tunnel through the rock to the place where the "real" mining starts

Beam engines – these were the steam powered engines used to pump water or raise ore from the mines.

The bob was the rocking beam of the engine

Calciner – the furnace for roasting the ore

Chimney (or stack) and flue – the flue took away the gases from the roasting process, impurities were deposited on the walls of the flue and the remaining toxic gases were taken to a "safe" height above the surrounding environment

Count House – the account house or mine office

Cousin Jack – a Cornishman who has emigrated to work in mining centres around the world

Dressing – this was the crushing of the tin ore (on the dressing floor) in order to facilitate its separation from the rock it is in.

Engine House – these are the square buildings with the big "windows" you see all over the place. The houses were actually an integral part of the beam engines since the giant beams pivoted and rocked supported by the ledges of the large apertures (the bob

walls) – the beam actually poked through this hole – the shaft of the mine being just in front of the engine house, They had to have incredibly thick granite walls to support the weight and the rocking of the beam (the largest of which, in cast iron, could weigh up to 35 tons) and the wooden pump rods attached to it (which could pump up to 2200 litres with one single stroke). The other walls were basically a brace for this main wall and also had apertures so the workers could get at the machinery for maintenance. It is because they were built so robustly that they are still standing today

They were often in pairs one pumping out water the other raising ore and raising and lowering men and equipment.

Lode – the seam containing the precious metals

Roasting – the heating of the crushed ore to burn off the impurities – sulphur and arsenic, especially

Wheal – Cornish name for a mine

Whim – those metal wheel contraptions for raising and lowering things down the mine

[13] Hot weather – If thermometer levels have stayed over 25 degrees centigrade for two days, then journalists will frantically begin scouring data and statistics for "the weather record". This is front-page headline material but to have any ooomph it must include the phrase "since records began" as in "Hottest early May bank holiday since records began." Another favourite ploy is to search out a foreign city particularly famed for its sunny climate, the closer the equator the better, that has had an unusually inclement 24 hours (or maybe they are in the midst of their winter, no matter) to be able to write "Heathrow hotter than Rio yesterday" If the situation continues for more than four days, then we are officially looking at a Heat Wave" – sometimes known as a sizzler (with the font perhaps jigging around as if frying). The headline, accompanied by people wading in a fountain in London, must include the phrase "as Britain melts"

True to form, once this longed-for set-of-events: set-fair, windless, hot weather, has arrived, and once the millions of fans for offices have been purchased, worries will immediately kick in as to the health risks of such high temperatures. The NHS will issue guidance to anyone at risk: the young, the old, anyone with pale skin and fair hair and anyone with breathing conditions. Headlines now will be "Air pollution reaches danger levels as pall of smog settles over London". "Pollen rates soar – bad news for hay-fever sufferers" Rain will be hoped for (if only for the garden)

Eventually, and most probably sooner rather than later, the sky clouds over, temperatures drop to "the seasonal average for this time of the year (i.e. cold). The entire population breathes a sigh of relief, relaxes and gets back to business as usual, and, of course, starts moaning about the weather again.

[14] Iron had several advantages over bronze in the arms department. Unlike bronze, an iron blade would never break in a clash of swords (bronze had a brittle side to it). In addition, it allowed longer swords to be made reducing the need to get up too close with your enemy. Iron was also cheaper to produce, and not being an alloy of two different metals, you avoided having two different supply chains that your enemies could disrupt.

[15] The Celts then were the self-same "Ancient Britons" that Emperor Claudius encounters in his definitive invasion in 43 AD. The expansion of the Roman Empire pushes them back to the western fringes – Scotland, Ireland, Wales and Cornwall. In Cornwall the new landlords dub them the Dumnonii. Later the farthest west region would come to be called Cornubia. At least 80 of the Dumnonii hill-forts still survive, such as Castle Dore just outside Fowey, or Treryn Dinas which guards the approach to the beach at Porthcurno.

The Romans establish a frontier stronghold at Isca Dumnoniorum (Exeter) in AD55, the base of the Second Augustan Legion. But – apart from a few isolated sorties – they don't venture further.

With the imposing bulk of Dartmoor standing in their way, a nice, straight Roman road would have been a massive undertaking. The Romans weren't good without roads. Also, though the natives were willing to trade in tin on their own terms, they were less willing to have their lands occupied. The type of guerrilla warfare involved in taking on these belligerent blue warriors (it was woad) on their own craggy terrain was not up the Romans' street. Doubtless, a centurion summed it up to his commanding officer with the Latin equivalent of a present-day Italian saying –"il giuoco non vale la candela". Roughly translated: "More trouble than it's worth, Sir".

Finally, a few titbits for those of a linguistic bent:

The Romans first coined the proto-type of the word Cornish, when they called the land east of the Tamar the pagus (district) of the Cornovii tribe.

Cornwall is actually a combination of Corn = horn (the shape of the peninsula) plus the Anglo-Saxon suffix wealas = foreigner.

The Celtic word for paint was brith and Brithon meant a painted man. Hey presto, here we are – the trusty Brits.

[16] The town is on the Camel estuary, and upstream is an area which has become famous recently for its wine production. The Camel Valley Vineyard is Cornwall's largest vineyard and has been producing wine since 1989. The business founded by Bob Lindo and his wife Annie, was later joined by son, Sam. They joined the big boys in 2010 in Verona when they beat the likes of Bollinger and Roederer to take the trophy in the Traditional Method Sparkling wine category. The company now have a Royal Warrant and produce wine "By appointment" for Her Majesty. A bottle of their award-winning Pinot Noir Rose Brut will set you back around £30.

[17] Joseph of Arimathea dealt in tin. He came to Cornwall with saffron to trade in exchange and various locations claim to be the place where he first set foot (possibly also with Jesus): St Just in Roseland near the church; at the Strand in Falmouth; Fowey has Punches cross which marks his landing spot. Looe also claims a visit and Joseph and Jesus can still be seen in their boat on the coat of arms of the town. Joseph apparently showed his metallurgical prowess by explaining to the locals a technique for separating the undesirable wolfram from tin ore.

After the crucifixion Joseph came to Britain in fear of his life because he had entombed Jesus' body and provoked the ire of the Sanhedrin. He built a chapel on the site of Jesus's Glastonbury home, a chapel seen by St Augustine sent to Britain by Pope Gregory the Great to convert the people to Christianity

[18] The blue colour came from woad. Woad was one of the reasons why the Romans after the invasion of Britain left the south-west well alone.

The leaves of this plant of the brassica family produce a blue dye. They are collected, dried in the sun, then ground into paste and left to ferment. This process, as well as releasing the precious dye, also liberates a terrific stench. It has been described as akin to a none-too-subtle combination of raw sewage and rotting cabbage. In fact, because of this, in Tudor times it was a criminal offence to prepare woad within 5 miles of a Royal Palace. Taking up the trade of woad-monger, bearing in mind that it took 50 kilos of the stuff to produce 5 kilos of pigment – was to accept a life as a social pariah.

Our forebears had a penchant, especially before battle, for painting their bodies with it. There were several quite good reasons for this.

For one, changing the colour of your body so that you and your men look like a squadron of extras off the set of Avatar is clearly going to have a disconcerting effect on your opponent.

Secondly, the plant extract had well-known antiseptic properties – in the case of a wound during the skirmish, you were already self-medicated.

Thirdly… there was that smell. For the sophisticated Romans, catching sight, and wind, of a marauding band of recently-emulsioned Cornovii would have been a daunting, and pungent, experience. Think posse of wild-eyed, indigo-coloured cage–fighters that has teamed up with a colony of polecats.

[19] In the fifth century inscribed standing stones tell us – in Latin for the most part – of Kings such as Mark and a son called Tristan. Men Scryfa, the Writing Stone, on the moors of Penwith, which talks of a famous local chieftain, also dates from this time. Then there is talk of a King called Arthur – who may or may not have existed. The starting point for the legend, Malory's La Morte D'Arthur was published in 1485 by Caxton. Caxton came to England in 1476 and one of the first things he published were chivalric romances, which culminated with Don Quijote in 1605 and 1615. Arthur is probably most interesting as an example of how men can be defined and/or created by words as much as by real experiences. Memes are powerful things.

Doubtless today there are Brexiteers out there who voted to leave Europe in the hope and expectation, nay the knowledge, that the country would as a result collapse politically, socially and economically leaving the field free for Arthur to ride forth from the groves of Avalon and lead the nation back to greatness.

[20] It was in fact, The Scillonian, on its daily run from Penzance to St Mary's in the Isles of Scilly.

The realisation of where Nancherrow actually was, also, in reality, happened in a slightly different way, if the truth be known.

I had finally gone back to the BBC Scotland documentary and realised that it had explained (a voice-over quote from Coming Home) that the view of the house on camera was in fact south-facing, and Pilcher, looking away from the house and slightly to her left says she can see the sea. So the house was on a south-facing stretch of coast.

Pilcher then walks from the house to the cove. She sits down and over to her left is an unusual rock formation jutting out into the sea. It is then that I realise that all the time I should have been searching for this geological feature, not the house itself.

Now, as we have seen with other locations, for example, Penjizal, Pilcher's descriptions of the journeys to the locations are very precise. Both Judith and Gus in Coming Home describe the journey from Penzance to Nancherrow, presumably travelling west as no mention is made of St Michael's Mount.

So off to Google Earth and it is not long before I find, along the south coast just past Lamorna, a rocky promontory similar to the one in the film. The problem now is that seen from above by satellite, it is difficult to tell if these are the same rocks as seen side-on in the film.

Then I discover the Geograph website – you type in any location and they provide you with a photo of the place. These are definitely the rocks.

Back to Google Earth, and, a couple of minutes later – up from the cove – Bingo! There is the garden. Now I move to Google images with the name of the house from the satellite map. Incredibly, it's still not the first to appear, but there it is, 3 or 4 pictures in – the house in the documentary.

Another couple of minutes and I have a name and a phone number for the house. "Would it be ok to take a couple of photographs for a book I'm writing?" "On Rosamunde Pilcher – your house is Nancherrow – it's in the documentary."

"Oh yes, I remember that – seventeen or was it eighteen years ago. I agreed to do it because I really wanted to meet Rosamunde Pilcher." "No, I don't want the name of the house in any publication. I don't want hordes of tourists coming round here." "I don't think she (Pilcher) had ever been here anyway. When we stood in the garden she didn't have a clue where she was (ed. – Pilcher would have been seventy-three years old in the doc of 1997 remembering back sixty years before). "So, no, sorry, don't mention the name."